THE JO

JERUSALEM

THE JOURNEY TO JERUSALEM

A Story of Jesus' Last Days

John Pritchard

WJK WESTMINSTER
JOHN KNOX PRESS
LOUISVILLE · KENTUCKY

Unless otherwise noted, Scripture quotations are taken or adapted from the New Revised Standard Version of the Bible, Anglicized Edition, copyright © 1989, 1995 by the Division of Christian Education of the National Council of the Churches of Christ in the USA. Used by permission. All rights reserved.

The publisher and author acknowledge with thanks permission to reproduce extracts from the following: 'The coming,' from *Collected Poems 1945–1990*, by R. S. Thomas (London: Orion Publishing Group, 2000), copyright © R. S. Thomas 1993. 'Welcome to the real world' by Godfrey Rust, from the book of the same title (Wordsout Publications, 2000) and online at www.wordsout.co.uk, reproduced by permission of the author. 'If Jesus was born today' by Steve Turner from *Up to Date: Poems 1968 to 1982* is reproduced by permission of Hodder & Stoughton. 'Father to the man' by John Knight from *Let There Be God* (Religious Education Press, 1968) is reproduced by permission of Elsevier, Oxford. 'Ballad of the Judas tree' by Ruth Etchells and 'A song for the tomb' by Teresa Morgan are reproduced by kind permission of the authors.

Every effort has been made to seek permission to use copyright material reproduced in this book. The publisher apologizes for those cases where permission might not have been sought and, if notified, will formally seek permission at the earliest opportunity.

Cover design: Eric Walljasper

Library of Congress Cataloguing-in-Publication Data
Names: Pritchard, John, 1941- author.
Title: The journey to Jerusalem : a story of Jesus' last days / John Pritchard.
Other titles: Bible. Luke, IX-XXV Paraphrases, English.
Description: Louisville, KY : Westminster John Knox Press, 2017. | "First published in Great Britain in 2014 by Society for Promoting Christian Knowledge." |
Identifiers: LCCN 2017042944 (print) | LCCN 2017043077 (ebook) | ISBN 9781611648409 (ebk.) | ISBN 9780664262693 (pbk. : alk. paper)
Subjects: LCSH: Jesus Christ--Passion. | John, the Apostle, Saint.
Classification: LCC BT431.3 (ebook) | LCC BT431.3 .P75 2017 (print) | DDC 232.96--dc23
LC record available at https://lccn.loc.gov/2017042944

♾ The paper used in this publication meets the minimum requirements of the American National Standard for Information Sciences—Permanence of Paper for Printed Library Materials, ANSI Z39.48-1992.

Most Westminster John Knox Press books are available at special quantity discounts when purchased in bulk by corporations, organizations, and special-interest groups. For more information, please e-mail SpecialSales@wjkbooks.com.

For Wendy, Sarah, Alison, and Gordon—faithful readers

Contents

————◆◆◆————

Contents

Week 4

Week 5

Week 6

Welcome to the journey

I've always loved the words 'Let's go.' They've invariably promised adventure: everything has been packed in the car for the start of vacation; the passports are in the bag; the newspapers have been canceled—'Let's go.' Or, we've finished lacing up our boots at the foot of a Lake District mountain; we've checked our backpacks; we've got the map—'Let's go.' For me, those words are always full of anticipation and promise. They're the trigger for action.

And so it was for Jesus.

For nearly three years, Galilee had been the main focus of his ministry. It was home turf. He knew and loved the way dawn crept silently over the lake. His heart warmed when he spied a field carpeted with wild flowers. The reassuring contours of the hills over the water, the greens and browns of the generous earth, the paths scratched purposefully between the modest villages—it was all his own familiar landscape.

But it was edgy too, in more ways than one. On the edge of Israel, Galileans were an independent-minded people, unhappy both with their Roman occupiers and the foreigners' Jewish puppets. Galilee was often on the edge of revolt. The bucolic serenity of the fields and orchards that sloped down to the shimmering lake was deceptive. It was a restless territory, always on the move, with traders traveling through from Mesopotamia with their heavy loads of cloth and spices on their way to the sea. But with their produce they also brought dangerous ideas.

In this abundant but uneasy context, Jesus had been brought up with his brothers and sisters. Joseph had taught him all he knew about the building trade, carpentry, and stonework.

He and his older brothers had most likely gone with their father every day to Sepphoris, the Roman town being built a few miles away, to ply their trade and earn the money that the growing family needed back in Nazareth. Their home village nestled in the valley a few miles from the lake, on the road to the great sea. It wasn't anything special, just a clutch of houses, each with its own vegetable patch and piece of land. There were probably no more than two hundred inhabitants.

But there Jesus learned not only lessons about wood and stone but also the lessons of God and destiny. He bided his time, but eventually he knew he had to make his move. It was like a compulsion within him, irresistible and awesome, something he could no longer deny was an overwhelming call on his life. He talked to his family, packed a small bag of food and water, and set off for the Jordan, where his cousin John was baptizing.

We know what happened then—it's in the Gospels. He taught and healed; he talked with people on the road and listened to their stories; he went out for meals and debated with his hosts; he told mesmerizing stories and chatted late into the night as the fire turned dark red. He gathered a group of young friends to travel with him. He made some enemies, but, to a much greater extent, he made friends and followers all over Galilee as crowds flocked to see the young, dynamic teacher whom everyone was talking about. And they weren't disappointed. He had a way of speaking that turned everything upside down in a way that made it seem the right way up. He cut to the heart of faith, bursting through tired ideas and pointless rituals. Sometimes he fretted over the slowness of people's response, but still he kept his patient program of travel, teaching, healing, and prayer.

Until the time came for him to turn toward Jerusalem and to say to his friends, 'Let's go.'

And that's where this book picks up the story. In Luke 9.51, there's a sentence that's easily overlooked: 'When the days drew near for him to be taken up, he set his face to go to Jerusalem.'

The rest of the Gospel account in Luke has to be seen in the context of that simple statement. He turned deliberately and momentously toward Jerusalem. The days of innocence, such as they were, were over. It was time to go to Jerusalem and put his message about the kingdom of God, now breaking into Israel's life, up against the religious politics of the high priests. It was a high-risk strategy, but until he took that step the crucial showdown was postponed.

I've taken nearly all the incidents on that journey and tried to enter into them with what Southern Baptists might call 'baptized imagination'. In other words, I've put my imagination to work within the framework of the story as Luke tells it. I've tried not to stray too far from what it is reasonable to imagine might have been the thoughts and feelings of the characters involved, but in the end it's informed imagination that I've been using. It's what preachers do every week to make the gospel come alive to their listeners; I've just developed the style a stage further.

I've chosen in nearly every section to tell the story through the eyes of the disciple John. I wanted someone close to Jesus, someone about whom we know a reasonable amount, and someone with whom I feel some empathy. John fits the bill, and on only two occasions do I leave him behind; he's young, he's still learning, and he has many years ahead in which to reflect on the significance of these three seminal years of his life.

I've written sections for each weekday of Lent, but I've used a poem for Saturday and left Sunday as a day of Sabbath reflection in church or elsewhere. But of course the sections can be used at any time of the year, not just in Lent.

At the end of each section I've used the technique of asking 'I wonder . . .'. This approach seems to me to open up many more possibilities of insight and learning than would more straightforward questions of fact or left-brain understanding: it allows us to ponder and ruminate; it opens up heart knowledge as well as head knowledge; it allows the imagination to come out to play and discover a deeper, integrated wisdom. But wondering requires a slower speed than that required for quick-fire answers to sharp questions. If you are reading *The Journey to Jerusalem* by yourself, please give yourself space to wonder, and if you are reading it as a group, then at the end of the book I offer some guidelines that might help.

I hope you're still with me. If so, welcome to the journey. 'Let's go.'

Ash Wednesday

Leaving home: Luke 9.51–62

I suppose we should have expected it. But even then I'm not sure we'd have realized how significant this moment was. We—that's me, John, and a group of friends—were getting ready to set off after breakfast, as we had done so often before, saying good-bye to our hosts and checking we hadn't forgotten anything, when Jesus called us together in the yard and said, quite calmly but looking each of us in the eye in that penetrating way of his: 'We've been here long enough. Let's head for Jerusalem.'

We nodded. We'd been to Jerusalem before of course so this wasn't too remarkable. But there was just something about the way he said it. James and I looked at each other. 'What's he really saying?' we wondered. Looking back we could see that he was setting off on the most important journey of his life, to see how the Temple intelligentsia, the top priests and the smart lawyers, would receive the message that had set so many hearts on fire in Galilee. Jerusalem had to be the final destination. Every prophet had to make his mark there.

But at the time, most of us just thought it was a five-day trek to Zion, the holy place that held our reverence and affection. It turned out to be a lot more than that; in a sense we never came back. We were young and, OK, we were naive as well. In retrospect, you can see it was bound to end in tears. (Or was it laughter? Just three days separated the two.)

So off we went that fine morning, with the sun sparkling on the lake and the olive trees gleaming silver-grey on the hillsides. We were an odd bunch in many way: two pairs of brothers,

1

Peter and Andrew, James and me; one or two of our friends, such as Philip and Bartholomew; and then there was Matthew, the former tax collector, whom we'd come to accept in spite of his past. We'd picked up Thomas along the way; he was a bit of a loner, who often wandered off by himself. And we found Judas to handle the day-to-day expenses. Simon, Jude, James ('the less' we called him, poor old James, to distinguish him from my brother, who was older). It was a great group. There were close and less close friendships in there, of course, but there was energy and fun and rivalry and endless chat. I loved it.

Jesus sent a couple of us ahead to let villagers know we were in the area and to ask if they could prepare some food for a small crowd coming their way. So it was more than a little disconcerting when our two came back, all hot and bothered, and told us we weren't welcome. Again, we should have known. We were going to head straight through Samaria, to avoid the long trek down the Jordan valley, and the Samaritans were always pretty hostile. How Jews and Samaritans could argue so passionately over which mountain to pray on always puzzled Jesus. He constantly drummed into us that religious things like the Sabbath were made for human beings, not the other way round.

James and I were furious at the rudeness of those Samaritans, who were rejecting the simple rules of hospitality. Remember, we were young; we had red hair and the temper that went with it. So we told Jesus he should summon fire from heaven to destroy this annoying little village. In our defense, Elijah had done something similar when King Ahaziah had proved particularly trying. But Jesus tore us off a strip, quite rightly. He reminded us that only a few weeks ago he'd sent us out to various villages to talk about the kingdom and (with wonderful trust) to heal people who were ill, and he'd specifically said that if a village didn't welcome us we should shake the dust of the place off our feet and go on to the next village.

James and I seemed to have forgotten that instruction. Somewhat ashamed, we dropped to the back of the group.

Days and times get a bit hazy. But on the early part of the journey it seemed as if a number of young people kept coming up and wanting to join us. It made those of us whom Jesus had already invited to join him feel special, because Jesus wasn't pulling any punches. One young guy was longing to join us, but Jesus said pretty bluntly that foxes and birds have got homes to go to but the 'Son of Man' (that strange title he kept giving himself) had nowhere to put his head down at night. He was right; we never really knew who would give us a meal and a bed for the night, which isn't surprising given what a crowd we were.

Another youngster had sadly just lost his father and not unreasonably wanted to bury him first. After all, that has top priority among our people. But Jesus was pretty brutal, if he wouldn't mind me saying so. 'Let the dead bury their own dead', is what he said. It was the same with someone who just wanted to say good-bye to his family. Jesus said that if you look back when you're ploughing, the furrow will go all over the place. He was right, of course, but he gave these would-be followers quite a hard time.

But Jesus knew what was waiting for us, happy innocents that we were. We were heading for a baptism of fire, a furnace, where every ounce of courage would be required of us. If we were to compromise at the start, we would cave in before the finish. He wasn't playing games. He was looking for total surrender to the cause of the kingdom. Why he expected this particular group of friends to deliver that level of commitment I just don't know. And we let him down so often and so spectacularly he must have despaired at times.

But it was still early days and we were still having the time of our lives roaming the paths of Galilee with this most amazing teacher and friend.

Jesus had only just turned his face toward Jerusalem.

Ash Wednesday: leaving home

I wonder what you might have felt if you had been setting off with Jesus that morning, heading for Jerusalem?

I wonder how you feel about those who reject the Christian faith?

I wonder how you feel about Jesus' strong words to those who wanted to delay a while to take care of their family duties?

I wonder what it is that holds us back from making the kind of commitment we'd like to make? What could we do to make that possible?

Thursday

The mission: Luke 10.1–24

It was a risk, and he knew it. In spite of doing his best to build up their confidence and give them some basic ground rules, sending out a crowd of seventy or so friends and followers, some of whom he'd hardly even gotten to know, was putting them—and him—on the line. They were to go on ahead to the places he would visit as he journeyed toward Jerusalem. They were the advance party. Nevertheless, he worried as he saw them go, some clearly feeling vulnerable and unsure, others jaunty and, if anything, overconfident. He watched them straighten their tunics, pick up their rough wooden sticks, and disappear down the various tracks away from the village.

He suddenly wanted to run after them and say, 'No, no, come back, let's talk some more. Maybe we'll be ready next week or next month or sometime . . .'. How could they possibly manage? Would they have the words? When someone said 'What on earth are you on about?' would they know what to say? Would all his teaching about the kingdom of God, the new world breaking in on them with its radical demands of love and justice, would that teaching have entered their hearts sufficiently to express itself clearly through what they said? When they sat by the bed of a sick child whose mother pleaded with her eyes for them to make well, would they have the faith to pray and rely on his loving Father? Or would their faith shrivel up and leave them mumbling platitudes? What had he done, sending them out like this?

But he knew that you only learn to swim when you get in the water. He had to trust. He had to believe that what he spoke about in terms of God working through our words and our touch and our prayers was not just true for himself but for all who tried to live in God's way with God's help. He had to let go.

The last pair disappeared round the corner of the path, and Jesus was alone. He sat in the shade and thought of what he'd told them. He'd said they'd be scared, sent out like lambs into a pack of wolves. Was that image a bit too vivid? He'd said they must be completely dependent on the mercy of God and the kindness of strangers. Shouldn't he have let them take a day's food, just in case? He'd said they should receive people's hospitality, cure the sick, and tell people that the kingdom of God was within touching distance. Shouldn't he at least have given them a script?

It's true his message had gotten a bit darker near the end. Those villages of Chorazin and Bethsaida had gotten under his skin. Even his own home town of Capernaum had been disappointing. It wasn't as if they hadn't seen what powerful things God can do when you let him. They had witnessed such things for themselves, and yet they were more resistant to the rule of God in their lives and practices than Tyre and Sidon, and that was saying something. But to be realistic, this was the last time he would be passing this way, and if the villages failed to respond to God's message of peace, then sadly there would be a reckoning. The stakes were high, and yet Jesus had sent out these young innocents to do the job. It was obvious why he was restless.

Time passed . . .

But when they returned it was like a group of schoolchildren coming back from their first week away from home. They were thrilled, laughing, joking, talking over each other, desperate to share what they'd seen and done. And Jesus, like a mother welcoming her brood home, was bubbling over too. He told them that what they'd done, he too had seen mysteriously in prayer; he'd seen Satan, the accuser, streaking down to earth, defeated by the power of God. And this, he thought to himself, is what it was all about, overcoming the terrible power of evil in the world, a huge undertaking he'd started in the desert when facing his own demons, and which he knew in his soul was a task he'd have to complete in Jerusalem. That's why he was going there.

Suddenly Jesus realized there was a danger attached to this joyful reunion. His friends could run off with the idea that they were the all-conquering heroes to whom the evil spirits submitted, and that wasn't the point at all. 'Rather rejoice', he said firmly, 'that your names are written in the Book of Life.' And that took Jesus into a reverie of prayer. They watched his face transfigured with a joy that struck them dumb. Whatever was going on was between him and his heavenly Father, but those closest to him heard his delight that God had given these wonderful, young, innocent friends of his such revelation and such amazing experiences.

He was exhausted; they all were. But he was good at celebrating. It would be a great evening.

> *I wonder how you might have felt if you'd been among those seventy brave followers sent out by Jesus?*
> *I wonder if you've ever done anything for God that really tested your trust in him?*
> *I wonder if there's anything lurking in your mind that God might be nudging you toward trying—something that requires more trust than you think you've got?*
> *I wonder what this story might have to say to our churches at this particular time?*

Friday

——•◆•——

Doing and being: Luke 10.25–42

It was strange being around Jesus. I could never work out how he came up with such brilliant stories. He did it again as we headed south. We were having a rest near a synagogue, sitting around the well, and up popped a lawyer who had obviously heard some of what Jesus had been saying to us. To this day I don't know if he was asking a genuine question or trying to trick Jesus, but he asked about eternal life and what he needed to do to get that. Jesus threw the question back neatly and asked the lawyer what he thought the answer was, to which this solid citizen of the law gave the classic response we all learned at school, about loving God and loving our neighbor.

But then the lawyer went a step further, and it's that that makes me wonder if he wasn't trying to trap Jesus. He smiled and asked innocently 'And who is my neighbor?' He probably knew that Jesus was pretty generous on this one—he didn't think in terms of some people being neighbors and others not, like the lawyer would. He always told us God's grace was much, much wider than we thought.

And then Jesus told this great story about a Samaritan (can you imagine?) doing an amazing rescue of a Jew who got beaten up on the very road we were heading for, the one from Jericho up to Jerusalem—only he was heading the other way. Understandably, both a priest and a Levite left the Jew alone, partly because it could have been a trap on this dangerous road and partly because a dead body was too unclean for these Temple officials to touch. Fair enough, but along came one of those obnoxious Samaritans, and he did everything he could

8

and more—bandaged him up, put him on his donkey, took him to an inn, stayed overnight to look after him, made an open-ended promise to the innkeeper when he left to pay for the man's lodging and other expenses. Way over the top.

Then came the killer question from Jesus: 'So who turned out to be a neighbor to the injured Jew?' Not 'Who should we choose to care for as good Jews?', but 'Who proved to be the caring person in an emergency?' Answer: one of the hated Samaritans! It was too much for our lawyer. It shattered his categories of who is and who isn't included among God's chosen people. He walked off quietly. James and I wanted to cheer, but Jesus gave us a look.

I can't quite remember when it was, but there was another time when Jesus seemed to be saying something opposite to this 'go and get on with it' message that he gave to the lawyer. This was when he seemed to be saying 'stay and listen to me' to his good friends Martha and Mary. They were friends to all of us, actually, but Jesus would sometimes go and spend a few days relaxing with them and their brother, Lazarus. They had something special together.

You'll have heard the story I imagine, Martha complaining that Mary was just sitting listening to Jesus when she, Martha, had all of us to prepare a meal for, and us strapping young men lolling around the courtyard and being generally useless. When Jesus said Mary had chosen the better thing to do, you can see why Martha might have been a bit put out.

But, you know, I think most of us misunderstood what was going on that afternoon. After all, Mary had done something rather shocking. She'd invaded the men's space in the house, the public room where only men met and talked, leaving the kitchen and other private rooms to women. So Mary was behaving as if she were a man—she'd crossed a big, invisible boundary in the house and in the way our society runs. More than that, she was sitting at Jesus' feet as disciples do when they're learning how to be rabbis. She was taking her place as a would-be teacher and therefore stepping over yet another really important line.

It was all rather scandalous, but Jesus accepted her right to be there. Afterward, Peter and I tried to make sense of it and thought it was probably a bit like Jesus saying the love of God can't be channeled in straight lines; it's like a river that breaks its banks and floods the whole countryside. I think that interpretation was lost on Martha, however. There was a frosty silence from the kitchen, along with a lot of banging of pots and bottles.

It seems to me there's a time to get up and do (like the Samaritan and Martha) and there's a time to sit and listen (like Mary). The secret is in working out which applies when. And if we were to ask Jesus 'Which one is better?' he would probably just say, 'Yes'.

> *I wonder which of all the characters in the parable of the Good Samaritan you feel you're most like?*
> *I wonder if society is getting more or less like the Good Samaritan in its response to need?*
> *I wonder what Jesus might have said to Mary and Martha the next day, when tempers had cooled a little?*
> *I wonder how much we 'get up and go' and how much we 'sit and listen'? Are we good at discerning which to do when?*

Saturday poem

'The coming' by R. S. Thomas

And God held in his hand
A small globe. Look, he said.
The son looked. Far off,
As through water, he saw
A scorched land of fierce
Color. The light burned
There; crusted buildings
Cast their shadows; a bright
Serpent, a river
Uncoiled itself, radiant
With slime.
    On a bare
Hill a bare tree saddened
The sky. Many people
Held out their thin arms
To it, as though waiting
For a vanished April
To return to its crossed
Boughs. The son watched
Them. Let me go there, he said.

Saturday poem: 'the coming'

I wonder which lines or images are the most evocative for you?

I wonder why the poet chose the phrases 'scorched land', 'crusted buildings', 'serpent', 'thin arms'?

I wonder if the son knew the bare tree was for him?

WEEK 1

---•◦•---

Monday

---•◦•---

Prayer: Luke 11.1–13

I used to love hearing him talk about prayer. It was as if we were eavesdropping on a lover talking about his loved one—almost embarrassing, but what a privilege. He would creep out before dawn sometimes, stepping carefully over the rest of us as we snored gently, dreaming of Galilee or, more probably, a big breakfast. And then he'd be gone, like a shadow in the mist, up into the hills where he could find, just for an hour or two, the peace and silence the rest of his life denied him. I was glad he did this, though it left me feeling that my own faith and desire for God was thin and threadbare in comparison.

One or two of us tried to copy Jesus a bit—we'd wander off and try praying quietly by a stream at the end of the day (if we weren't on duty preparing food—we had a strict rota). But it was never long before someone would come charging over to discuss some hare-brained scheme or to challenge us to a race of some sort. In any case, prayer outside the synagogue or away from the Sabbath meal seemed slightly odd, even a little embarrassing, if I'm honest.

But we could see that prayer was the source of Jesus' life, the energy that filled him and enabled him to keep listening and loving and talking and touching, when I for one was almost screaming for people to go home and leave us alone. How did he do it all? This was how—prayer. Sharing everything with his Father, laying it all before the God he trusted absolutely, with every pore and particle of his being.

One day we were sitting by a river. We'd finished a somewhat meagre lunch of bread dipped in olive oil, when one of us—I can't remember who—asked Jesus to teach us to pray. I think we'd heard that Jesus' cousin John had taught his followers a kind of 'team prayer', and we wondered if we could have our own. Jesus had been over in a field praying by himself while we relaxed in the sun, and it just seemed a good time to ask.

So he taught us a prayer—you probably know it. It clearly came straight out of Jesus' own way of praying. It even started in that really intimate way Jesus addressed his Father. He called him 'Abba', would you believe? Dad. Daddy. Wow, so close up. We loved that prayer. It became our theme song; we'd say it before we set off for the day's travels and when we stopped by a gurgling stream for lunch or gathered in the evening to plan the next day. We were soaked in that thin and threadbare prayer.

Another thing. Jesus gave us the prayer in Aramaic. We were used to prayer being in Hebrew because we thought of prayer fitting in a sacred, liturgical context, but here was Jesus placing it right at the heart of our own familiar daily life. Prayer suddenly became truly personal; Aramaic was our own language. The prayer sounded like this: '*Abba, yitqaddas semaj, tete malijutaj . . .*'. We loved it.

But Jesus gave us some other little gems. One story I heard him use a few times in teaching different groups was about a man who found he didn't have any food for someone who'd just turned up at midnight, and he goes to a friend who's all tucked up in bed and asks if he can have some bread. And the friend grumbles for a while but eventually gets up and gives him what he needs—Jewish hospitality and all that.

The first time I heard that story I was a bit puzzled. We have to persuade, cajole, wear God down to get him to answer our prayers? Surely that's not what Jesus meant. Then I realized he was saying if that's what we humans are like *how much more* will God come immediately to our aid? It's all in that contrast; 'how much more?' So ask, and it will be given; search and you will find; knock and the door will be opened.

That's what I believe now too. Not that it's been easy. And we certainly don't always get what we want. Enough of our merry band has gone to glory prematurely to counteract any fantasy about God having favorites that he'll look after, come what may (I do miss James and Peter). But no prayer is ever not used by God, simply because no love is ever not used by God. And prayer is our best way of loving. I'm not claiming to understand the ways of God in the ways of the world, but I know they're interacting all the time. I know that the world is soaked in God and God is soaked in the world, and that God is always building and shaping a kingdom of such justice and joy that when the time comes we'll be struck dumb by its beauty.

But I'm getting carried away. What I meant to say is that I learned so much by seeing how Jesus' life was utterly rooted in prayer and the pleasure he had in his relationship with his Father. I've never forgotten it—though I still don't really know how to do it and experience it. I keep trying.

So nearly every day I go back to that team prayer that we so enjoyed and that we taught to everyone: 'Our Father in heaven, hallowed be your name . . .'. I hope that someday it'll be spoken in every language in the world.

> *I wonder if Jesus had enough time to pray?*
> *I wonder if Jesus expected that millions of people would pray*
> *'through Jesus Christ our Lord'?*
> *I wonder how you've coped with the problems of*
> *'unanswered prayer'?*
> *I wonder what form of prayer you find most helpful, and*
> *what you'd like to do to develop your praying further?*

Tuesday

———•◦•———

Demons: Luke 11.14–32

It was irritating to say the least. Jesus had been helping someone who couldn't speak and it was lovely to see the delight on his face when he uttered his first sounds. There was a stream of people coming to see Jesus for help; so many of them had some disease or disability that was messing up their lives. To be honest, sometimes it was overwhelming. I would see Jesus at the end of an evening and he looked white with exhaustion. As they kept coming with all their different ailments, I sometimes felt like saying, 'Please go and heal yourselves. We just can't manage all of you.' But Jesus never weakened. He simply listened and loved them, touched and healed them. It was astonishing to watch.

So you see what I mean when we were irritated that some of the sceptics said Jesus was dealing with the demons behind these illnesses by the power of Beelzebul. They couldn't ask whether the healings were really happening—the evidence was in front of their eyes—but they could ask who was doing it. Beelzebul meant Baal the Prince, a local god hostile to the true God of Israel, an agent of Satan. So here was the best of men being accused of being a servant of the worst of evil. It was so frustrating. The work was difficult enough without this silly nonsense. What they'd spotted of course was that Jesus didn't do these things like other exorcists. He didn't pray in the normal way, using our traditional Jewish liturgies. He simply commanded things to happen, on his own authority. He told the demons to go—and they went. To some people, I admit, this was worryingly direct. To them, he seemed to be claiming an authority that wasn't his, so in that sense, their question was valid: by whose authority was Jesus doing these things? Who was it who was healing these people?

Jesus stood up wearily and knocked down their argument in three rapid strokes. One: why would Satan work against himself? He would lose the battle automatically. Two: were his opponents also to be charged with being agents of Satan? If not, why should Jesus be charged with that? Three: look at the facts—Satan might be strong, but if the finger of God himself is at work (as I tell you it is), then even the strong man in his heavily guarded castle will be defeated and his goods plundered. It was interesting that he used that image of the 'finger of God'. My mother used to tell me the story of Moses trying to get our people out of Egypt, and as a boy I loved the plagues of frogs, gnats, flies, boils, locusts, and such like. It was wonderful, lurid stuff to listen to at bedtime.

But I remember that phrase that pharaoh's magicians used when those plagues proved unstoppable. They said it was the 'finger of God' doing these things, doing the impossible. So now Jesus was doing these things as the agent of the kingdom of God—the kingdom that had come upon them, which was even now hovering over them, filling them with a new energy. That's what you're seeing here, said Jesus.

The opponents looked a bit discouraged. They knew they'd been beaten. Jesus returned to the queue of people who longed for him to do just what he'd been saying and deal with whatever it was that was destroying their health. But then Jesus paused, as if he'd just remembered something else he ought to say. He called to the small group of opponents who were just leaving the courtyard where all this was going on. 'One moment,' he said. 'Do remember that if you clear a bad spirit out of a person but don't fill up the space with good, then a lot more harm may come pouring back in; seven evil spirits may take up residence in no time.' He was right: an empty house invites intruders. When we were kids in Capernaum, we couldn't resist creeping into houses that had become empty and exploring them or making dens in them. Sometimes, I fear, we made quite a mess in there.

Suddenly a woman in the queue to see Jesus couldn't hold back any longer. 'Blessed is your mother to have produced such a boy as you!' she said. But Jesus came straight back with 'Blessed even more are those who hear what God's saying to them and act on it!' It sounded like a bit of a put-down, but the woman took it in good part. She saw the grin on Jesus' face, and she nodded. 'I agree,' she said.

A little later Jesus had a lunch break. We insisted on it. We could see more and more people arriving, and we knew we had to protect Jesus from himself. And that's when we got into an odd conversation with him. He must still have been thinking about what the woman had said and how he'd answered. It was the response that people make to God's Word that mattered, he'd said to her. People have gone seriously off track when they always say they're looking for a sign, but don't obey the Word of Life when it comes. Jonah's preaching was a sign that the people of Nineveh should repent, and they did, much to his surprise. If the people of Nineveh listened to that comic figure who got stuck in a whale, shouldn't the people of Israel be even more ready to listen to an authentic voice even greater than Solomon?

Jesus was musing. It was a puzzle why some received the teaching of the kingdom with obvious relish and others ignored or opposed it. What more could he do?

Time would give the terrible answer.

> I wonder what you understand by all the talk in the Gospels about demons, unclean spirits, and so on?
> I wonder what place healing has today in Christian proclamation?
> I wonder what are the best ways to deal with scepticism and opposition to the Christian message?
> I wonder what you do when you feel overwhelmed by people's needs?

Wednesday

———◆•◆•◆———

Confrontation: Luke 11.37–54

Sometimes Jesus was so embarrassing! One particular evening stands out in my mind. I don't know if he'd been in an argument with someone or if he'd simply gotten out of bed on the wrong side. (Not that we had beds very often—we usually lay on mats or straw mattresses packed close together, hoping no one would roll onto us in their sleep.) Anyway, we were having a meal with one of our Pharisee acquaintances. This happened quite often. After all, Jesus and the Pharisees had a lot in common: they worshiped together in the synagogue every week and believed many of the same things about their faith. Indeed, a short while later it was a group of Pharisees who came to warn Jesus that Herod was out to kill him.

So Jesus wasn't an outsider attacking an institutionalized religion. He was an insider who loved the Jewish faith. But this time he really laid into the Pharisees, even though our host was one himself. With just minimal provocation (our host expressed surprise that Jesus didn't wash in the approved manner before dinner), he virtually accused the Pharisees of being clean on the outside but filthy inside. He called them fools. He said that they gave their due in tithes and the produce of the land, but they didn't do anything about vital issues like justice and the love of God. He said that they loved to show off in the synagogues and marketplaces, but they treated ordinary people with contempt. Ouch! It was pretty excruciating to watch.

Of course he never liked hypocrisy. But now that he was properly worked up, he just got on a roll. A lawyer remonstrated with him. Now lawyers were often called scribes because they were

19

trained in writing legal documents, so they were strong on precision and maybe a bit weaker on compassion. Well, this lawyer probably wished he hadn't gotten up that morning. Jesus accused him of laying burdens on ordinary people and then watching them struggle, and then he virtually accused him personally of having killed most of our ancient prophets!

Jesus got so angry about all this that he realized he'd gone too far, socially, and with a word of apology he went outside. You could have heard a pin drop. No one quite knew what to say, but gradually our host and his friends found their voices and began to complain bitterly about this aggressive behavior and breach of etiquette.

Peter and I talked about it later, and we began to wonder whether Jesus' anger was about something more than moral outrage at the hypocritical actions of his fellow teachers and the lawyers who backed them up. Perhaps it wasn't so much that Jesus was contrasting a religion of hundreds of petty rules with a religion of love and grace, as that he was contrasting a religion that focused on law as the motivating principle with a religion that recognized the need for profound national repentance. He saw the need for our nation to turn away from its deep, prolonged rebellion against God—and against Rome for that matter, which confused the issue even more and would inevitably bring the vengeance of Rome down on us.

Whatever it was that brought on that outburst, it helped us to see the passion in Jesus' mind and heart. He wasn't a fluffy do-gooder, and nor was he a political terrorist. He was utterly focused on God and the hope of the kingdom. I think he sometimes simply got frustrated that as a people we had so much within our reach and yet we continued to saunter aimlessly toward oblivion.

I found Jesus later on. He was calmer then, looking out at the hills beyond the village; familiar, friendly shapes in the darkness. I put an arm around him, and he looked at me and smiled a little sheepishly. 'They didn't like that much, did they?' he said.

'Maybe not', I replied, 'but sometimes things just have to be said.' 'Thank you,' he said, and moved off into the night.

> *I wonder whether your place at the table would have been with the host and his friends or with the disciples? And if with the former, how would you have felt at this meal?*
> *I wonder where the agenda of Jesus most clearly confronts the agendas of the wider world today?*
> *I wonder what we are doing about the agendas that make Jesus angry?*
> *I wonder where the Church has gotten itself on the right side of these issues and where it has gotten itself on the wrong side?*

Thursday

Warnings: Luke 12.1–12

Our journey to Jerusalem was a strange affair. Sometimes it was full of high spirits and fun—after all, we were a group of young men, friends; some of us had known each other for years. And we had more energy than we knew what to do with. I'm a bit embarrassed to remember our more robust games and the tricks we played on each other. Embarrassed because of what must have been going through Jesus' mind as he looked beyond us, toward Jerusalem. After all, he knew what it was all for, why we were going there, while we just thought it was the next stage in a marvelous adventure.

But sometimes we caught a glimpse of the seriousness of the journey. There was one time, for example, when we'd stayed for a couple of days in a pleasant spot among the hills, and word had gotten around that Jesus was there, so people had begun to gather to hear what he had to say. I never understood how it happened, but before you knew it a little group had become hundreds, maybe even thousands, each finding a spot on the hillside where they could settle down and listen to this exciting young teacher.

But while they were gathering in their hundreds and we were looking on in astonishment, Jesus decided to call us together, just the twelve of us, and began speaking to us urgently about being careful of what we said, because what we thought was just between us would inevitably be heard by everybody. Word always gets out and what we thought was secret would soon be public knowledge proclaimed from the housetops. If we were to gossip about what we hoped Jesus would achieve, you could be sure it would get to Herod's ears and we'd have his soldiers after us.

I looked around at the earnest young faces focused on Jesus. What a mixture: Peter—bearded, strong, solid Peter—the one you always wanted near you in a tight spot; Matthew—older than the rest of us, more experienced, wise, grateful; Thomas—thoughtful, watchful, but absolutely loyal (I really enjoyed my conversations with Thomas); James—my faithful brother, fellow explorer of life, ginger hair always in need of a brush; Judas—I always admired his quick mind and his ability with numbers and money; and yes, the rest of them. These were my friends. All of life was before us, and Jesus was our guide.

But the crowds were still arriving from all directions, so Jesus carried on. He talked about not fearing Herod or even the Romans, because finally we answer to God alone. But this God, who holds our destiny in his hands, is the one who knows us so well he even knows how many hairs there are on our heads (even in Peter's beard, I wondered?). So I was reassured; God knew and loved us down to the last detail. And then came one of those moments when the conversation lurched into a dark place.

I want your loyalty, Jesus said, and his eyes burned with intensity as he held each one of us in his gaze. If we stayed loyal to him before other people, he would be loyal to us for all eternity. But the opposite was also true: if we were disloyal we were on our own. And although forgiveness is always available to everyone, if we or anyone tried to make out that good is bad and bad good (he mysteriously spoke of this as 'blasphemy against the Holy Spirit', but I think I got the sense of it all the same), then we would have cut ourselves off from the very possibility of recognizing truth or possessing life. I shivered.

But Jesus did at least give us one reassurance. He said that if we were on trial for our loyalty to him, we would be given the words we needed to defend ourselves and to bear witness to our beliefs. That at least was some comfort.

But as I looked up at the blue sky and hundreds of expectant faces turned in our direction, I felt a shadow pass over my soul. This was serious business we were talking about on this sunny hillside, but did we have any idea just how serious? There was a new tension inside me as I watched Jesus begin to speak to the crowd. There's dedicated opposition out there, far beyond our innocence. There are problems up ahead that are going to need us to be really focused and deeply loyal.

Was I up to the challenge that Jesus was throwing down?

> *I wonder how you would have felt hearing these warnings at first hand? Would you have wanted to continue on this journey?*
>
> *I wonder what the disciples thought was going on as they went to Jerusalem?*
>
> *I wonder how much you see faith as a good part of your life, with real spiritual and community benefits, or as a serious and focused following of a dangerous but life-giving savior?*
>
> *I wonder if you have ever experienced being given the right words when called to account for your faith?*

Friday

Possessions: Luke 12.13–34

I used to love it when he told us stories. Actually, that's not quite true; there were times when the stories seemed to be directed straight at me, and they stung. But generally I loved it because those stories cut right through to the heart of an issue we were discussing and suddenly I could get it, or if I couldn't get it immediately, the story would bug my mind like an itch until the coin dropped and I got the point.

It was like that, once, when Jesus was teaching about something—the kingdom probably—and a young man in the crowd couldn't contain himself any longer and called out that Jesus should tell his brother to divide the family inheritance with him. He must have been the younger son, and there can't have been a will, because the law said in such circumstances the estate couldn't be divided until the older brother agreed. So he had a legitimate complaint, and Jesus was usually red hot on issues of justice.

But clearly Jesus wanted to go deeper. I can see him now, looking straight at the young man in the kind of way that could make you feel quite uncomfortable. When he'd decided how to respond, he said, 'OK, here's a story.' He described a successful farmer who didn't do anything wrong in the way of mistreating his workers, nothing illegal or unjust. He simply lived his life completely turned in on himself. He didn't see that his wealth wasn't a right he deserved, but a gift he'd received. He didn't think to share his wealth with others; he just thought he needed to build bigger barns to keep all his crops safe. He even (and I liked this touch) talked to himself about what he should do, and no one does that where we live; we always talk every-thing over with family and friends. We live together in our communities, and we chat endlessly around the supper table, deciding together what we should do. So this farmer in Jesus' story was really odd, thinking only of *his* crop, *his* barns, *his* good, *his* soul. The only person he consulted was himself.

But that doesn't work. Ultimately you can't keep God out of the picture. So God's voice thunders in—'You fool, this night your soul is required of you. And these things you've collected for yourself and kept safe, whose will they be now?' It was a great finish.

And then we had one of those 'Jesus moments', where he just tossed in a single sentence that had us scurrying for safety. 'That's what it's like for those who store up wealth for themselves but aren't rich in their relationship with God.' Brilliant. Even I got it. And so did the young man, judging from his expression. The problem of economic justice isn't sorted out by saying 'I want what's mine.' We need to go deeper and look at the issue of justice from the perspective of ultimate ownership—who really owns everything? Our life, and everything in it, is on loan from God. We have to curb our perpetual desire for 'more', or it destroys us.

Never one to lose an opportunity, Jesus widened the discussion, because he realized that most of us don't have the problem of too much wealth, but we do have the problem of too little, and we get anxious. It was one of the great things about Jesus' teaching that he was always in touch with the basic realities of life. He was really down to earth, and he made God down to earth too. So he knew that lots of us just had only enough to live on, with only one spare shirt, for example, and food for only a short time. And we worried that the family breadwinner could become ill or get injured and then we would be in real trouble.

So he began to encourage us to look behind that anxiety and see if we could trust God with our needs. He said that birds and flowers could teach us a thing or two because they just got on with what they had to be, and God took care of them. He was at his most poetic this time, talking about lilies that don't work for their beauty but are more glorious even than Solomon, and yet it didn't come across as romantic sentimentality. He was absolutely practical, pointing us unerringly to the greatest priority of all—focusing on the kingdom of God and then trusting that God will see to our needs because he loves us. It was both so logical and so difficult.

And then another of those 'Jesus moments', a phrase so telling that I wouldn't be surprised if people aren't still saying it hundreds of years from now.

'Where your treasure is,' he said, 'there your heart will be also.' Ouch!

I wonder what the young man might have done next?
I wonder where our treasure really is?
I wonder how much we trust God with our needs?
I wonder if it's hard to share any good financial fortune we may have had in our lives?

Saturday poem

'If Jesus was born today' by Steve Turner

If Jesus was born today
it would be in a downtown motel
marked by a helicopter's flashing bulb.
A traffic warden, working late,
would be the first upon the scene.
Later, at the expense of a TV network,
an eminent sociologist,
the host of a chat show
and a controversial author
would arrive with their good wishes
—the whole occasion to be filmed as part of the
'Is This The Son of God?' one hour special.
Childhood would be a blur of photographs
    and speculation
dwindling by His late teens into
'Where Is he Now?' features in Sunday magazines.

If Jesus was thirty today
they wouldn't really care about the public ministry,
they'd be too busy investigating His finances
and trying to prove he had Church or Mafia
    connections.
The miracles would be explained by
an eminent and controversial magician,
His claims to be God's Son recognised as
excellent examples of Spoken English
and immediately incorporated into
the GCSE syllabus,

Saturday poem: 'If Jesus was born today'

His sinless perfection considered by moral philosophers
as, OK, but a bit repressive.

If Jesus was thirty-one today
he'd be the fly in everyone's ointment—
the sort of controversial person who
stands no chance of eminence.
Communists would expel Him, capitalists
would exploit Him or have Him
smeared by people who know a thing or two about God.
Doctors would accuse Him of quackery,
soldiers would accuse Him of cowardice,
theologians would take Him aside and try
to persuade Him of His non-existence.

If Jesus was thirty-two today we'd have to
end it all. Heretic, fundamentalist, literalist,
puritan, pacifist, non-conformist, we'd take Him
away and quietly end the argument.
But the argument would rumble in the ground
at the end of three days and would break out
and walk around as though death was some bug,
saying 'I am the resurrection and the life . . .'
No man cometh to the Father but by me.'
While the magicians researched new explanations
and the semanticists wondered exactly what
He meant by 'I' and 'No man' there would be those
who stand around amused, asking for something
called proof.

I wonder how many of the poem's assumptions you agree with?

I wonder what the implications are of Jesus being born when he was?

I wonder what of today's world, and what of the Church, Jesus would most applaud and most condemn?

WEEK 2

Monday

Disaster and penitence: Luke 13.1–9

Sometimes I just longed for everyone to stop talking. There were so many words. Jesus taught wonderfully, but then people wanted to come and tell him their life story or beg him to sort out their health, or their children, or their mother-in-law. Some came to argue, some to chide, some to warn. But day in and day out, it was words. And, incredibly, all the time Jesus was encouraging us, looking after us—preparing us I suppose. And healing people! So sometimes I just wanted peace; time to play games on the lake shore, time to cook food on the beach as the sun went down, time to be young and carefree. Occasionally, Jesus insisted that we went away for a holiday retreat. Once we went way up north to Caesarea Philippi and another time to Sidon on the Mediterranean coast. Those were good times.

Jesus had a great gift for looking after us. You'd be walking along deep in your own thoughts, and suddenly there'd be an arm round your shoulder: 'How's it going, John?' And he'd listen. Listen to how I felt, leaving the family behind, wondering how dad was managing without us, missing mom's home cooking. He cared. And you felt you were the only person in his life at that moment.

But we always came up against reality again before long. I remember a rather earnest couple of men who came to tell us about the latest outrage that Pilate had committed. Pilate really was a loser. He was unpleasant and unpopular, and sometimes it seemed as if he was simply trying to wind us up. He had no sensitivity for a start. He once tried to bring some Roman military standards, with all their pagan symbols, right into the holy city. Another time he used Temple money to build an aqueduct and then crushed the rebellion that resulted. He rode roughshod over all our laws and religious traditions. And now this: the two men told us that some Galileans had come to Jerusalem on pilgrimage and as they were sacrificing in the Temple Pilate had thought they were going to riot, so he sent in the troops and slaughtered them.

Maybe these two messengers were asking Jesus if he still wanted to head to Jerusalem with a madman like Pilate around, but Jesus responded with a different kind of question. Did they think these Galileans were any worse than other Galileans to deserve that cruelty? And while we're about it, did they think that those eighteen poor people who were killed when the tower of Siloam fell on them were any worse than the rest of us? I wasn't sure where Jesus was going with this. Perhaps he wanted to challenge the widely held view that if something bad happens to us it must be because of some bad thing we've done in the past. Sin causes suffering. I'd never been very convinced by this way of thinking and was glad to hear Jesus undermining it. I'd seen enough good people suffer and enough rogues get away with it and prosper.

But in any case this wasn't really where Jesus was going with his line of thinking. Any attempts to correlate sin and suffering, he said, distracted us from the main issue, which is our obligation to live before God in both penitence and trust. Unless we repent, all is lost for all of us. This kind of humble living before

God isn't linked to life's joys and sorrows; it's our deepest call. Actually, this is one of the things I admired about Jesus—the way he didn't spare either God's mercy or God's judgment. He didn't merge them into an anaemic compromise; he said both were full, red-blooded elements of God's character. So we all, as a nation and as individuals, needed to repent, and then we'd find that the mercy and love of God were limitless.

He went on to illustrate what he'd been saying with another of his parables. (We ought to have had someone writing these down, they were so helpful. Fortunately we had good memories for stories.) He told us about a man talking with his gardener about a fig tree that had produced nothing, so the owner said to cut it down. But the gardener asked for one more year and to give it special treatment before making that final decision. We knew the code: owner equals God, fig tree equals Israel, gardener equals Jesus. (Or it could have been owner equals Jesus, fig tree equals Israel, religious leaders equals gardener. Who knows?) The trouble is Jesus never wanted to explain these stories but simply let them stand or fall by their own persuasiveness. But it didn't matter here because, either way, the call to repent and live before God trustingly and obediently held true. The fig tree wasn't doing its job, and something had to change. Someone had to repent. But would we?

So again it hadn't been a quiet end to the day. It was hard thinking all the way, with lots of words. But it was my turn to do the cooking that night, so I could putter about the fire without having to think too much. I didn't think the fish would argue.

> I wonder if people still think deep down that if bad things
> happen to them it's because they've done something
> wrong and God or fate is punishing them?
> I wonder how disturbing it might have been to be part of
> Jesus' team of followers?
> I wonder how the Church can use the word 'repent' today?
> I wonder whether we take penitence seriously?

Tuesday

———•◦•———

The healing business: Luke 13.10–17

Synagogues are powerful places. People get very intense. Down on the beach, when we were still fishing, we often used to say that too much religion was a bad thing; it needed to be kept under control. But then along came Jesus one sunny morning and blew our prejudices to pieces. Here was something quite different, fresh, exciting, dipped in light. So it wasn't a great surprise when we went to the synagogue one Sabbath and there was a bit of a bust up; the old religious ways were suddenly confronted by this new style of faith that we were seeing in Jesus. It happened like this:

Our home village, Capernaum, had only a few dozen houses, but inevitably it had its synagogue set in the middle, reminding us that though there could only be one Temple (in Jerusalem) there could be any number of synagogues in the villages and towns of Galilee and Judea. So in we went, as usual. The first problem for the synagogue committee was how to cope with the arrival of this dynamic young preacher, who people wanted to see. The president of the synagogue was officially in charge, but all eyes were on Jesus. So there was a bit of a power struggle right from the start. Not that Jesus wanted it; it's just that that was the effect he always had.

Anyway, they showed a bit of wisdom that morning and let Jesus preach. The rest of us were quite relaxed, glad to have a break in the shade, because outside the sun was blistering hot. Jesus was in full flow, much to everyone's delight, when an elderly woman crept in upstairs, where the women had to go. She was cruelly bent over. People moved away, keeping their distance. It turned out she'd been like that for eighteen long years, twisted and brittle so that you'd think she would snap if you touched her—but nobody did.

Jesus spotted her immediately though, and you could see that he was appalled at her state. He stopped mid-sentence and called to her, asking her to come down. Poor woman, she was so embarrassed: bad enough to be bent over and in permanent pain, with people assuming she must have done awful things in her youth to deserve this punishment; now she was going to be paraded in front of everyone too, like an exhibit.

We knew better, of course, and sat up. He had something in mind. Always did. He ran his hand down this poor woman's back and said with that deceptive simplicity of his, 'Dear woman, you're free. Walk tall.' Or something like that. And there, before our eyes, we saw her unbend and slowly lift her arms above her head, all the time stammering words of delight and gratitude, her face lighting up like a girl in love! We grinned. Everyone clapped.

Well, not everyone. The leader of the synagogue had a face like thunder. He turned to the people and started to harangue them, tearing them off a strip for coming to be healed on the Sabbath. Strangely he didn't seem to be able to address Jesus; he took it out on the crowd. Perhaps Jesus was just too much, too powerful, too *complete* maybe. Anyway, this pompous guy in charge went on and on, saying the people could come and work, or be cured, or do anything, the rest of the week but the Sabbath was a holy day when nothing like this should take place. Suddenly Jesus was on his feet again, clearly deeply upset. He looked at the leaders with a mixture of sorrow and distaste. 'You hypocrites!' he said, with a force we didn't hear. 'You set your ox or donkey free on the Sabbath, but you won't allow the same freedom to this old lady who's been bound in this terrible prison for eighteen years!'

What he was pointing out was that all of us kept at least one ox or ass in our houses overnight, but in the morning we all, without exception, untied them to take them outside during the day. We didn't have stables; we had very basic houses with a lower floor or cave for our animals. But of course the animals had to be freed during the day, even the Sabbath day, and even if you were leader of the synagogue. Jesus had hit the spot.

Well, it was mayhem that morning. The synagogue committee shrivelled up, and the people were delighted at what they'd seen, stamping their feet and applauding. Jesus meanwhile was talking with the old woman, his arm around her straight shoulders, smiling again.

Much later on, as we talked over episodes such as this, we saw that something else had been demonstrated that morning. What Jesus had done for that poor woman was what he longed to do for the whole of Israel, to set her free from her rigid rules, her exclusiveness, her oppression of the poor. His message of the kingdom was the great explosion Israel needed to free her from her slavery to conservatism.

We didn't see it then of course. There was a lot to learn first, which was often painful. What we did see, however, was our teacher walking out of the synagogue, side by side with a free woman.

> I wonder what might have happened in that synagogue after that memorable day? I wonder what might have happened to relationships in that tight-knit community, and how the elderly woman got on?
> I wonder what restricts our churches from being the places of freedom and hope that they're meant to be?
> I wonder if there are situations and people that God is setting before us at the moment, as churches and as individuals, to set free?
> I wonder where we personally feel bound and in need of the liberating touch of Jesus?

Published on Nov 22, 2014
A tribute to a true saint of our age :) Click 'Show more' to s

Just as I am, without one plea,
but that thy blood was shed for me,
and that thou bidst me come to thee,
O Lamb of God, I come, I come.

Just as I am, and waiting not
to rid my soul of one dark blot,
to thee whose blood can cleanse each spot,
O Lamb of God, I come, I come.

Just as I am, though tossed about
with many a conflict, many a doubt,
fightings and fears within, without,
O Lamb of God, I come, I come.

Just as I am, poor, wretched, blind;
sight, riches, healing of the mind,
yea, all I need in thee to find,
O Lamb of God, I come, I come

Just as I am, thou wilt receive,
wilt welcome, pardon, cleanse, relieve;
because thy promise I believe,
O Lamb of God, I come, I come.

Just as I am, thy love unknown
hath broken every barrier down;
now, to be thine, yea thine alone,
O Lamb of God, I come, I come.

Wednesday

---◆•◆---

The fox and the hen: Luke 13.31–35

You have to remember we were all quite young. Matthew was a bit older of course and had seen a bit of life and how it worked. Judas was quick too, and Thomas always struck me as very thoughtful. But most of us were working lads from around the shores of Galilee, and suddenly we were finding ourselves mixed up with some pretty heavyweight, educated characters with legal and religious backgrounds. Sometimes we struggled with this new world.

So I certainly don't want to be too hard on the Pharisees. Yes, some were self-righteous prigs, but others of them seemed genuinely interested in what Jesus had to say, and some, like our great friend Paul, became passionate supporters. So it wasn't a surprise when three of them turned up one day with real concern for Jesus' safety. 'Herod's out to kill you,' they said.

Now Herod wasn't exactly a supporter. But then none of us were his supporters either. In fact we thought he was a nasty piece of work, smug and self-indulgent. He had his little bit of authority in Galilee only because the Romans had admired his father as the best thug around. So Jesus gave his Pharisee friends a wry smile and said something which at first was reassuring but became chilling.

He sat them down on the grass and said, 'Go and tell that sly old fox that I have a job to do and he should get off my back. The work of the kingdom has to go on today and tomorrow and on the third day it'll be finished.' Then he looked down at the coarse grass and said more quietly, 'Yes, today and tomorrow, that's fine, but the next day I'll have to be in Jerusalem because that's where prophets have to be killed.'

There was an awkward silence. None of us could think what to say. But Jesus had begun to speak enigmatically about this 'third day' quite a bit recently. At first we thought he meant to remind us of the story his mother used to tell us, of when he was a child and got left behind in the Temple at Jerusalem and when they found him three days later he quite calmly told them there was no need to be anxious—he was bound to be in his Father's house. And him a twelve-year-old! Mary used to chuckle at that memory.

But now this 'third day' had popped up again, and it seemed to be tied up with his death and maybe something else as well. We didn't want to hear all this. I shuffled my feet in embarrassment. Peter looked about to argue back until a swift glance from Jesus stopped him in his tracks.

Then Jesus stood up and stretched, but his mind was obviously far away. He spoke wistfully as he looked toward the south. 'Jerusalem, Jerusalem,' he said, 'you who kill prophets and stone those who bring hope. How often I would have loved to have gathered you up as a hen gathers up her brood of chicks, but you wouldn't have it. . . . Why, my little ones, why?'

He was in a kind of reverie. We couldn't join him there, so we watched, helpless. I looked at Peter, but he was just as stunned as the rest of us. Here was a glimpse into the emotional world of Jesus as we made this long walk to Jerusalem, and it was painful to watch. This was a whole other dimension of our extraordinary friend, who usually kept us entranced by his conversation, so lively, so honest, so full of laughter, fond of good company and a glass of wine. But this was when the curtain twitched and we caught a glimpse of the cost to Jesus of the mental struggle that must have been going on.

I felt unsteady for a moment, as if the air had been sucked out of me. What was going to happen in Jerusalem? What was this gut-wrenching desire to gather up chicks like a mother hen protecting her brood? I remembered my parents telling me once of a hen being found after a farmyard fire. She was dead, scorched and blackened, but under her wings was a little collection of live chicks. Did Jesus see himself taking the full force of some impending disaster, trying to protect us by giving his life? I was horrified.

But the sun still shone high overhead. The birds were in high good humor. The excited shouts of children playing in the stream floated toward us. It sounded so unreal, all this gloomy talk. James and Andrew walked by, tough fishermen who knew how to haul in heavy nets or to protect a friend from attack. But who would want to attack such a good man, anyway?

I shook myself back to normal and went to thank the Pharisees for their warning. We would be careful, I said. There was quite a gang of us, all fit and strong and ready to defend Jesus. Peter, over there (I nodded toward him), he would give his life rather than let any harm come to Jesus. Don't worry, I said.

But thanks anyway.

> I wonder what Jesus' friends really thought was going to happen in Jerusalem? I wonder why they thought they were going there?
> I wonder how Jesus lived with those thoughts and fears of what might or would happen when they got to Jerusalem? How much did he know or guess?
> I wonder how best we should travel with friends and loved ones who have seemingly insurmountable problems—as the disciples traveled with Jesus?
> I wonder how you cope with your deepest fears?

Thursday

———◆·◆·◆———

Table talk: Luke 14.1–24

It was astonishing how much Jesus could achieve over a meal.
I'm surprised he ever got invited back, such was the controversy
he sometimes caused. One occasion I'm thinking of was a meal
with another of the Pharisees, who found Jesus an interesting
person to talk to. I was lucky enough to go along with Jesus,
and I could see how much he enjoyed these occasions, with
good food and stimulating conversation. He was quite jaunty
as we arrived, even though you could see that there was some
tension in the air; after all, Jesus had charged some of them
with hypocrisy, and he in turn had been accused by them of
playing fast and loose with the law.

But Jesus greeted our host warmly and was settling down
onto the cushions when a man with quite severe swelling in
his legs dragged himself in. In our country the doors are left
open when we eat, so anyone can wander in: beggars, relatives,
or simply curious passers-by. And of course Jesus healed him;
it just came naturally to him. But he sensed the familiar dis-
approval around him (it was a Sabbath), and he was clearly a
bit irritated to have to point out that if it had been one of their
children who'd accidently fallen into a well, they might actually
have stretched a point and got the child out.

We moved on. Or at least I thought we had, but it seemed that
Jesus was almost looking for trouble. I could see him watching
the guests coming in and eyeing up the seating arrangements,
then making for the best seats. Jesus told them that that was
a very risky thing to do, because if someone truly important
arrived they would have to suffer the embarrassment of being

moved down to the lower seats, whereas if they went for the humbler seats in the first place, they might find themselves moved up higher instead. Good advice.

Only we all knew that wasn't what Jesus really meant. He was having a dig at those who were well off and legally trained and wanted to push themselves forward in the sight of God, assuming superiority and the best seats in the kingdom. Not so, he was saying; you'll be in for a surprise. Much later, as I remembered this incident, I wondered whether Jesus wasn't also laying the ground for a kingdom where not just Jews but Gentiles also would be welcome, a fact which at first some of our brothers and sisters who came from a Jewish background found hard to accept.

So now could we sit down and eat? Apparently not. Jesus wanted to have a word with the host about not inviting these local worthies to banquets at all, but rather those who couldn't return the invitation and were truly in need of generosity— people like those favorites of Jesus, the poor, the crippled, the blind, and so on. You could understand why our host was getting a bit tetchy; he wanted to get on with the meal, not be lectured on the values of this 'kingdom of God' that Jesus kept going on about.

At last Jesus made his way back to the cushions. I was ready to get my teeth into something substantial; our meagre lunches of bread, sometimes fish, and water from a stream were hardly body-building for a group of young men. But wouldn't you know it, one of the dinner guests decided to become all pious, so Jesus went into storytelling mode and again we had to delay getting into the dishes of cheese, hummus, olives, eggs, fish, and various meats that were laid out before us. We listened. Ah yes—it was this one; I'd heard it before. About this man's banquet, when all the smart people who had accepted the invitation sent excuses when the reminder came. Interestingly, the excuses weren't unreasonable—they'd bought land or oxen or just got married and in other societies those reasons would

41

have been quite legitimate. But this invitation was urgent and not to be dismissed that easily. So the servants were sent out into the town and eventually into the countryside to fill up the empty places with the poor, the maimed, the blind, and the lame.

I wondered at first if the assembled company got it, and then of course I remembered they were bright Pharisees, many of them, and they understood very well. They were being told they were foolish to refuse the invitation to God's great banquet and that God was inviting all kinds of social outcasts—foreigners, slaves, bonded laborers, Samaritans, prostitutes, beggars, and assorted low life—to fill up the table of hospitality instead of them.

All these points were wonderfully made of course, but they didn't exactly endear him to many of the guests. Some were intrigued, but there were a lot of scowls around the low table. I couldn't help wondering where all this was going to lead. If Jerusalem was going to be something of a showdown, as I increasingly saw it might be, then Jesus was going to need all the friends he could get. And this wasn't getting him them.

But Jesus was enjoying himself. As he settled down to eat, he smiled genially at everyone and then asked innocently, 'So who's going to say a blessing on the food?'

> *I wonder how the meal might have gone after that?*
> *I wonder if Jesus was angry or trying to provoke?*
> *I wonder how you would have felt meeting Jesus if you had been a good, religious Pharisee?*
> *I wonder who is excluded from our church life? I wonder who we don't notice?*

Friday

Costly discipleship: Luke 14.25–35

As we continued our journey to Jerusalem we had become quite a crowd, mostly on the young side and single, but some were in families, and there were even some older women who I think were helping to pay for everyone's food and accommodation. But it was hard to tell what kind of a crowd we were. For instance, were we a parade, out for a good time, waving our banners for Jesus and oblivious to any cost this might entail? Or were we a march, protesting against the religious and military authorities, and preparing for a clash: Galilee versus Jerusalem, Jews versus Romans, Jesus versus the establishment? In some ways it did begin to look as if it was peasants versus power, a kind of northern rebellion.

I wondered if we weren't really a sort of death march, but with Jesus the only one who was actually facing this possibility. The rest of us were high on hope and the fun of it all, though we were increasingly realizing there was serious business to be done.

Anyway, there came a moment when Jesus decided to bring the issue out into the open. We were up in the hills and had just stopped by a stream for a rest. The sun was beating down, and the path was stony and bruised the feet. Some of us were paddling in the stream, others sitting in the shade. Jesus leaned against a tree and asked us to gather round.

He started speaking, gently but firmly. He was clearly moved by the enthusiasm and loyalty of everyone, and he thanked us. But then he said that if we were to go with him all the way it would mean putting this loyalty above everything else—above parents, above family, even above the preservation of our own lives. We Jews have a vivid way of speaking sometimes, and we exaggerate, so it sounded as if we were to 'hate' our families and our own lives, but we understood what he was saying—it was all or nothing, and were we ready for that? We would have to detach ourselves from many other good and important things if we were to see this through.

What 'this' was, of course, we still couldn't know, not even Jesus.

The crowd was very still by now. This was a crucial challenge: he was talking about the cost of following him to Jerusalem—it wasn't a Sabbath afternoon stroll. He used two images to emphasize the need for thinking it through. He probably had in mind the wonderful new Temple Herod was building in Jerusalem when he said if you're going to build a tower, you have to work out how much it will cost first or you'll end up looking very stupid if you run out of money. And if you're going to go into battle, you have to work out whether you have a fair chance of success. As I look back, this was an odd example, because any rational calculation of the odds stacked against Jesus in going up to Jerusalem and pitching himself against the Romans and the Temple authorities had to look desperately one-sided. But who knows? Maybe Jesus thought the people would rise up with him or that God would sort it out in some way. Anyway, there it was. We failed (and succeeded a thousand times over!). But I'm getting ahead of myself.

I looked around at the crowd of good, uncomplicated, hopeful people who had joined us by this stage of our journey. And some faces were now looking troubled. This was worrying talk. Some young men were exchanging glances with their wives—we even had a few children with us; we could hear them playing happily in the stream. Some of the adults were looking steadily at their feet and clearly weighing things up.

Jesus looked at us again, his face giving out a dozen messages at once—tenderness, desire, anxiety, seriousness, regret, love. I saw it all. He was struggling to be realistic, but he so loved the world he was leaving as Galilee slipped behind us. And he loved to bits these good people who were following him. He didn't want to put them off and send them home, but at the same time this was a dangerous path and he knew that only the seriously committed should attempt it. He even used the image of it being like carrying your own cross to your death, and he couldn't have given a more vivid illustration of how focused and determined we would need to be.

We lost a good number of traveling companions that day. And they were right, they were doing the correct thing. Everyone had to make their own lonely decision about what they could manage. The twelve of us who had the privilege of being Jesus' special friends on this journey were becoming increasingly aware that we needed to be stripped and ready for action. The kingdom of God was not an easy win but a great battle, and Jerusalem was the battleground.

We watched our friends leave, all of us sad but understanding. I had an uneasy sense of things closing in on us. And then we picked up our packs and turned once more toward the holy city.

Jesus, his face inscrutable, was in the lead.

> *I wonder what the crowds who returned home might have been thinking and feeling as they left?*
>
> *I wonder what Jesus might have been thinking and feeling as he turned back to his journey?*
>
> *I wonder if you've seen people turn back when the cost of discipleship became too high?*
>
> *I wonder if you've also been tempted to turn back, and why?*

Saturday poem

'Father to the man' by John Knight

I warned the parents, you know,
when he was a child. I said

This boy really must not be allowed
to argue about the law with lawyers and about God
with theologians. And he seems, I said,
to fancy himself as a doctor, too. At this rate
we shall have him, perhaps, giving water
to a feverish patient. Little thinking
he'd do just that; and was lucky
the lad recovered.

It will come to no good, I said.
But one gets no thanks.

And so it went on
until, later, we lost touch;
for he was away for some years,
no one knew where.

Afterwards, I admit, I was half convinced. More than half,
I suppose I should say.

When he preached—and I shall hear no such sermons again—
it seemed that immutable right and wrong—
no, it was not that their boundaries changed. But somehow
acts and facts seemed with a shake of a word
to fall—I saw such a toy once, of foolish beads—
in a different pattern. What was done was the same,
and right and wrong were the same, and yet
not the same, being done in a different world.

46

Saturday poem: 'Father to the man'

There was a wedding, for instance,
with, in plain Aramaic, too much drink,
and you know the country customs—
I fear the old Gods are by no means dead.
Well, he was there, and he preached on the Sabbath,
and spoke, just in passing, about the wedding;
and, you know, these junketings (to call them no worse)
seemed transformed, seemed a part
(like David's dancing in the Temple)
of our holy religion; and,
what was stranger, our religion
seemed to have grown, and to be our life.

Well, you see, it has come to no good,
as I told his parents, children
must listen, and lawful authority speak.

. . . and yet
this is the saddest news . . . and I
am nearer to death . . .

I wonder which words or phrases caught your attention the most?

I wonder what is meant by 'acts and facts seemed . . . to fall . . . in a different pattern . . . being done in a different world'?

I wonder if you experience, or have ever experienced, your religion to be your 'life'?

I wonder what makes us feel nearer to death?

WEEK 3

Monday

Lost and found: Luke 15.1–32

It was one of those afternoons I'll never forget. We were sitting around the well just outside the village, enjoying a rest and a drink after a day in the hot sun, when we found we were being joined by a steady stream of locals. And gradually we realized that most of these locals were actually the village outcasts: the simpletons, the tax collectors, the street women. And of course there were also some of the grumbling Pharisees who complained that Jesus attracted only sinners and other forms of low life. He even ate with them, they said—as if that proved anything.

But what made that afternoon so special was the stories he told. I don't know when he thought these stories up; they simply seemed to flow out of him at will. He perched on the side of the well and just started. There were stories of a lost sheep and a lost coin and then a lost son—or one who seemed to be lost but then was found—and his brother who seemed to be found but was actually lost, because he couldn't tell the difference between being lost and being found. Or he was both—or neither. I think. If I'd understood it right . . .

Because you had to work at these stories he told us; he didn't always finish them off for you, or smooth off the rough edges. For instance, this young lad who ran off with his father's money, he was a real tearaway, not someone any of us would have felt sorry for. By taking a third of his father's wealth (the younger brother's share) while his dad was still alive, he was kind of saying 'I wish you were dead.' By changing his property into money, he was dishonoring the land that God had given to all of us as Jews. By squandering the money on wine, women, and song he was showing himself to be right outside our law. By hiring himself out to a Gentile, he was showing his contempt for the covenant we had as a nation with God. It was a spectacular list of failings.

And yet the father runs out to him. Runs! For the father of the household to run like that was utterly demeaning. And in any case had this degenerate young man really repented when he returned, or had he just realized which side his bread was buttered? That's what I mean by Jesus not smoothing off the rough edges. There was a lot to keep thinking about.

Another example. What about that loyal, hard-working older brother, didn't he have a legitimate complaint? He got up before dawn, worked hard all day, took no money out of the farm, and never had a party thrown for him and his friends. He had to ask one of the slaves in order to find out what all the music and dancing was about when his brother returned. His parents hadn't even thought to tell him. It was the music and dancing that sounded truly offensive. All right, penitents can be restored, but where does it say that they have to be thrown an expensive party? It might be acceptable to have the renegade return, but surely to bread and water, not to a fatted calf. Let him come in sackcloth, not the finest robe; let him wear ashes, not a fancy ring; let him come in tears, not with laughter; let him come kneeling, not dancing.

Now, deep down I know what Jesus meant. He meant that all our little calculations, our trivial attempts at spiritual accountancy, our doing good and trying to deserve God's love, all of this was redundant in the light of the reckless, outrageous love God has for every single human being. All of us wear the smudge and stain of messy lives, and our little spiritual games simply break in pieces in the face of God's liberating passion for forgiving us and letting us flourish. In a sense it was all one in the eye for the narrow Pharisees over there under the tree; they were like elder brothers grumbling over the party Jesus was throwing for these ne'er-do-wells. But Jesus himself wasn't vindictive; he just wanted people to see how much, how very much, they could trust God's love for them no matter what they'd done, or however much they'd written themselves off. I suppose grace is always offensive: we find such generosity hard to believe; and we find it hard to accept that God doesn't put people into boxes like we do—older son or younger son, saint or sinner, publican or Pharisee, Jew or Gentile. God's love is all-inclusive, not either/or.

So I know what Jesus meant. But he sailed so close to the wind! He told these stories right under the hot gaze of the Pharisees, and he never flinched. They must have winced as this powerful preacher told these subversive stories so fluently and passionately. They must have felt things slipping out of their control.

So I suppose we should have seen it coming, what happened in Jerusalem. But at the time we just enjoyed the thrill of it all.

And in the meantime we were left with all the loose ends of the story. What would the elder brother do now? How would he get on with his younger brother when they met? What would the father do to hold the family together? And why wasn't the boys' mother in the thick of it? And most of all for me—did I see myself in the loving father, or the messed-up younger son, or the offended older one? Or in all three?

51

The truth is, that story still gets under my skin.

I wonder what the various characters might do now to take the story forward—including the mother?

I wonder which character you most identify with, and why?

I wonder who it is that our society finds it hardest to forgive?

I wonder if there's anyone waiting for you to open the gate of forgiveness and throw a 'welcome home' party?

Tuesday

I have to admit, sometimes I just didn't understand. Things happened so fast in those amazing three years that I didn't always get the chance to follow up something Jesus had said and ask him to explain it. In fact Jesus often didn't want to explain his stories anyway; he said they either made their point or they didn't, so explaining them was a bit like explaining a joke. But I would still love to have sat down and had a chat with him about some of the things he said.

For example, there was a story he told us about a dishonest manager who was facing the sack for shady dealing, so he reduced the debts owed to his master in order to curry favor with the debtors and be in their good books when he was unemployed. So far so good, I thought, the manager was a crook and would be punished. But no, the master commends the manager for being smart! Well, I ask you—was Jesus saying that a bit of sharp practice was a good thing? I could hear messengers taking the news throughout Galilee: 'Celebrity preacher commends dishonesty.'

I stretched out on the grass and tried to think this through. OK, I knew that money lenders often added the interest onto the capital at the time of a loan so that they couldn't be accused of usury, which was a sin of course. And the agent would usually add his commission on as well. So the manager here might have been striking out his commission in order to make friends with the debtors while not defrauding his master. But if that was all there was to it, why was the manager called dishonest?

I also suspected—arrogantly perhaps—that the story wasn't really about money at all, but about Israel being unfaithful and unreliable with the stewardship of God's covenant. I say this because whenever Jesus or any of the great rabbis talked in their stories about masters, or pieces of land, or managers and tenants, you knew they were actually referring to God and his people. So here in this story we had Israel being unfaithful and getting caught out, and then trying to sort out the mess as well as possible. So the message to Israel was: 'Don't be unfaithful, but be as wise as the children of this worldly age so that you can face the oncoming crisis of the kingdom that's almost upon us.'

Two flies landed on my face. I shook my head and sat up. Were any of my musings anywhere near the mark, or was I just putting my best interpretation on an impossible puzzle? Was I trying to save face for Jesus because it looked like he'd gone off the boil for a moment? I tried to focus back on what he was saying. He'd gone on to a story about a rich man who lived royally on his vast income while a poor man called Lazarus was dying at his gate; covered in sores, gaunt, hollow-eyed, and famished. Immediately I felt to be in more familiar territory. I'd known this kind of story since I was a child. It was about the kind of reversal that happens when God's around, or in Jesus' terms, when the kingdom of God is in place. When the two of them die, it's Lazarus who's looked after by Abraham, and even when the rich man asks for his brothers to be warned about what might happen to them, Abraham says they've had warning enough.

I sank down onto the grass again, because I saw another problem, even with this familiar old story. Didn't our Scriptures say again and again that obedience to God's commandments led to God's favor and therefore to wealth? A fragment of the law floated into my mind, 'If you obey the Lord your God, blessed shall you be in the city and blessed shall you be in the field. Blessed shall be the fruit of your womb, the fruit of your ground, and the fruit of your livestock. . . .' So the rich man must have been obeying God's commands, surely?

But then I saw why Jesus insisted he wasn't trying to do away with the law, but rather to interpret it properly and fully. What the rich man was doing was obeying one part of the law, the outward part, but missing entirely all that Moses said again and again about our responsibility to the poor; the harvest was to be shared with the needy and the transient. Another piece of Scripture floated in: 'Is this not the fast that I choose, to share your bread with the hungry, and bring the homeless poor into your house. . . .' This was where the rich man had gone wrong.

I got up and wandered off down the path, looking for a quiet place to sleep. All this teaching sometimes made my head ache. It was exciting, certainly, but on a hot day, when we'd already walked for four or five hours, what I really needed was shade, a cold drink, and a couple of quiet hours before supper. It was someone's birthday that day, so there'd be a special meal, chosen by the birthday boy, and some great banter as we ate. There might even be singing and some of Peter's mad games. But all that could wait. . . .

I wonder what Jesus' hearers would have made of the story of the manager who acted dishonestly?

I wonder if we might have to think of Jesus a little differently if he could tell a story like that of the dishonest manager?

I wonder if Jesus was a bit hard on the rich?

I wonder how we can move beyond all the words we say about caring for the poor and actually do it?

Wednesday

———◆◆◆———

Closing the circle: Luke 17.11–19

It was horrific. There we were, getting close to another village, when a whole gang of them came over the hill. They hopped and limped and swung their leprous limbs. Their faces, arms, and legs were covered with lumps and bumps and white blotches. It was awful. They looked hunted, desperate, scared. Of course, lepers had to keep away from the rest of us, so they got together in colonies but kept near the main routes, so they could beg. As they struggled closer you couldn't help but look away.

Except Jesus didn't. If I remember correctly, he got up and walked steadily toward them, arms out as if receiving a gift. Perhaps to him they were a gift. It always amazed us how he sort of hummed with life when undesirables came near. It wasn't how we felt, I can tell you.

I couldn't quite hear all the conversation, but I did hear Jesus say to them, 'Now off you go and show yourselves to the priests.' I knew what that meant. If they were to be formally declared healed, they would have to be given that release officially by the priests. That was the law.

The trouble was, they hadn't been healed; they were still lepers, all blotchy and crippled. But such was Jesus' . . . what was it? Authority? Power? Persuasion? No—*connection*—such was Jesus' connection with them that they went hopping off, still on crutches, painfully limping their way back to the synagogue that they'd been barred from for so long. They trusted him.

They hadn't gone far before I heard the first shout. It was a whoop really, a cry of amazement and joy. Then another, and another. We stood up to see what was going on. What had looked like a crab crawling unhappily over stony ground had become more like a lizard moving fast and true, heading for home.

But then I noticed that one figure had peeled off from the rest and was coming our way again. He was a big man, but he moved like a boy, or perhaps like a man who'd just discovered he was a boy. He kept feeling his face with a look of amazement, and he gazed down at his feet as if they'd just appeared.

He came up to Jesus in a state of wonder, thanking God over and over. He knelt down at Jesus' feet, and then, as if that wasn't enough, he prostrated himself. But Jesus reached out, lifted him up, and hugged him. The man kept on saying 'thank you' with a gratitude that seemed to be drawn from the very depths of his being.

Jesus hugged him again and then, surprised himself, looked at the man. 'Isn't it odd?' he said. 'Weren't there ten of you a moment ago, and yet only one—you, good friend—have come back to thank God. Isn't that odd?' At first I thought, come off it; you told them to go and see the priest and that's what they're doing. But then I thought, 'Yes, he's right.' There's always time to give thanks. Indeed maybe giving thanks is part of the healing.

As Peter and I talked about it later, we realized there were two quite different things going on here. As we saw it, nine of those poor people were cured—fixed, if you like—but only one was healed. Only one understood what had really happened. And then we remembered something else that was important; that man was a Samaritan! So technically he was a social outcast and a religious heretic. How come he had the insight to know what was really going on? Indeed why did this happen so often? Peter asked. Why was it outsiders who got it and us Jews who missed it—missed the deeper stuff that Jesus was talking about? It was as if we Jews had gotten so familiar with being God's own people that we'd lost the wonder of it, but when these outsiders experienced the touch of God they were blown away.

I was delighted they were all sorted out physically and socially, but I was even more delighted that one person closed the circle and reconnected with the source of his new life. He'd recognized the presence and action of God in his life.

And I think this is one of the main things we got out of all the amazing events that happened around Jesus. We began to see the presence and action of God all over the place. Life's full of amazing things. What's not amazing about the first cry of a baby, all wet and scrunched up from the womb, or the fierce energy of a storm on the lake, blowing up from nowhere? What's not incredible about someone saying they love you like no one else in the world or about opening your eyes in the morning and seeing all those ravishing colors again?

Of course life's full of these miracles, but what being with Jesus taught us was to recognize the presence of God in all these things. We saw not just the goodness of the world, but the Godness of it. We began to see divine fingerprints everywhere. We began to see connections, indeed to realize that everything and everyone is connected, and connected above all to God. We were coming to see that everything is a gift from the hands of a God who loves us more than we can begin to imagine, and that we only become who we truly are when we make that connection, when we close the circle. That's what healing means.

And that's what our newly healed friend had begun to realize. It was just the start of a journey for him, but his intuition was telling him that what he needed most deeply was a new intimacy with God. And that's what Jesus confirmed when he spoke to him again. He just said, gently but firmly, to this newly made person before him, 'Now go on your way, but remember that it was your faith that healed you fully.'

Spot on. To be fully healed we need to be in touch with God. And in a deep, exciting way, not just formally. Gradually, I think I'm learning that too.

*I wonder what might have happened to the other nine
when they got home from the synagogue?*

*I wonder if you've ever felt like a leper—excluded, outside
the circle?*

*I wonder what reminds you of God's presence in the midst
of ordinary life?*

*I wonder if, when, and how you've let Jesus touch you with
his life?*

Thursday

The coming of the kingdom: Luke 17.20–37

There were times when Jesus looked deeply preoccupied. Not depressed quite, but in another place, sometimes a dark place. So I'd sit down beside him, give him a friendly nudge, and say, 'How's it going, boss?' He'd smile, wryly. I had no special right to do this, but somehow it felt like my job to look out for him. To imagine what it must be like for him, living with all that responsibility. He seemed to appreciate it anyway. 'Nothing that a jug of wine can't sort out,' he'd often say. So I'd fetch it and we'd chat about Galilee, our brothers and sisters, the fishing business, and the olive harvest. I think it helped.

But Jesus was nothing if not resilient. Peter and I were sitting chatting after lunch. I can't remember what we were talking about, but we became aware that Jesus had been cornered by some of the Pharisees. Now some Pharisees were friendly, remember, but we were always a bit on our guard when they rolled up, so Peter and I wandered over innocently to listen to what was going on.

We got there just in time to hear one of them ask Jesus when the kingdom of God would come. Belief in the kingdom of God was common ground between us. We all longed for the full reign of God to come, and while there seemed to be no detailed plans available, we had images of peace, freedom, and prosperity in our minds. Jesus sensed this wasn't a trick question but a genuine inquiry, and I was pleased to see that these well-schooled religious leaders actually wanted to know what our semi-qualified teacher thought about these things. Good for them—a bit of humility at last!

So Jesus took the question seriously, and Peter and I were all ears too, because we wanted to know if we'd get some warning of when the kingdom might come. But Jesus was very direct; don't look for clues, he said, don't follow every wild theory and crazy premonition. And then he said something really quite elusive. At first we thought he'd said the kingdom of God was within each one of us, but then we realized he couldn't be saying that, not when he'd been as frank as he was about some of the colleagues of these Pharisees. What he was really saying was that the kingdom of God already existed between us, it was in our midst, it was present when we lived according to our true nature and calling.

But that posed as many problems to Peter and myself as the other interpretation of what he meant, and as the Pharisees dispersed, I could see that Jesus realized he could again be misunderstood. He called us all together. Some were washing up, some having a rest in the grass, others were playing with a group of local children. But Jesus wanted to clear up what could be the source of a major confusion. Put simply, if the kingdom of God was already here among us, what about the full arrival of the kingdom in the future? We'd got the impression that what we were seeing with Jesus was a kind of 'front edge' of the reign of God and that the full works would appear later. The kingdom was both now and not yet, here and still to come. Had we got that wrong? Was the kingdom here already? Were we not still waiting for the Main Event?

Jesus reassured us. He gave us a scary but still hopeful picture of the kingdom coming to us at some unknowable time in the future, like lightning in the night. There won't be time to pack a bag or finish ploughing the particular corner of the field we're working on. It'll take our breath away, just as it did with Noah, picnicking happily in a field beside the Ark, or Lot, leaving Sodom after a day at the market. Suddenly their lives changed forever. So it will be with us. And it will be decisive for everyone: two people in the same bed, one taken, the other left;

two women preparing a meal, one taken, the other left. ('Which is which?' whispered Peter to me. 'Is it best to be taken or left?' I said I didn't know—but let's hope we're still wherever Jesus is.)

But in the midst of this vivid picture that Jesus gave us he made a comment, almost an aside, which not everyone picked up. Maybe we just didn't want to hear it, but it was definitely there. He said the Son of Man (his code for himself) would have to suffer badly and be thrown out by the present generation. How could this be? It was really unsettling when Jesus said things like this. Peter got very upset and started shaking his head. But there it was: we couldn't dismiss it; we couldn't forget it; we just had to hope it was something Jesus had gotten wrong.

The problem was, that would be a first.

> *I wonder how the disciples might have felt after this kind of conversation—alarmed or reassured or what?*
> *I wonder how literally Jesus might have thought all this was going to happen?*
> *I wonder what we should do with this kind of passage?*
> *I wonder what you think a sermon on these things should say?*

Friday

Prayer and justice: Luke 18.1–8

I've always loved stories. All Jewish children are brought up on a rich diet of stories that come from our faith, some of them inspiring, some of them puzzling, some that I rather wish weren't there—Jael hammering a tent peg through Sisera's forehead comes to mind. But it always seemed that we lived in a sea of stories, and we became very good at remembering them; if we couldn't remember all the details of the law, we could at least remember the stories of Abraham and Isaac and Jacob, of Moses and Joshua, of David and Solomon, the kings and prophets, and later, the heroes of the revolt against Rome and so on. Our minds were crammed full of fascinating people who had done brave, faithful as well as silly things.

So it wasn't surprising that Jesus told so many stories when he taught us about the kingdom of God that was breaking into our lives. What was more surprising perhaps was the way so many new stories came pouring out of him at a moment's notice. I can't imagine when he thought them all up, but there they were, ready for the moment, and we remembered pretty well all of them, I think. But here's another important thing about Jesus' stories—they often seemed to have a number of different levels at which they could be understood.

For example, he once told us a story about a judge who was a bit of a thug. He didn't seem to respect either God or other people. A widow kept coming to see him, day after day, seeking justice over some issue or other, and the judge kept sending her away. He had to tell the servants to say he was out of town. But still she came. Sometimes he even hid in a back room or on the roof to get away from her. But still she came. Eventually he gave up, heard her case, and gave her the justice she deserved because, he said, she simply wore him down. So, said Jesus, if it was like that with a judge who was a really difficult character, how much more quickly would the God of justice and compassion come to the rescue of those who seek help? God's very character is Justice and Love, so we could rely on him being completely on our side if we needed his support and vindication.

Now, Jesus was often preoccupied with this issue of vindication. He was anticipating that God would justify those who were faithful to the true meaning of our religion, and defeat those who were corrupting it. I tremble to think of it now, but sometimes I had the temerity to suggest that he might lighten up a bit on the Pharisees and the scribes because they had a job to do, and while they often got it wrong, they often got it right as well. Jesus would smile at me and agree with some of my simplistic analysis, but he said the stakes were very high, that God was on the move and desperately wanted his people back. The religious systems had become rigid and oppressive and fatally compromised and God's kingdom was being offered as a top to toe corrective. But this new life and transformed faith was being opposed all the way down the line by the religious and political powers. God would vindicate those who were open to his renewal, but not as a reluctant judge, rather as a devoted Father.

You know what I said about the different levels of Jesus' stories? Underneath the sharp message of this particular story about the unjust judge was a lovely message about the character of God and the nature of prayer. We learned so much from Jesus about prayer. It had always seemed pretty formulaic, confined to synagogue and ritual prayers on the Sabbath. But Jesus had opened up to us a whole new world of prayer as a natural conversation with the God who loved us like a father. I listened to him talking about prayer once, and I felt as if I'd been dipped in God and made new. Prayer was a loving relationship, not a dull duty. We could go to God at any time as a child to his Abba, and we would be swept up in his love for us, though he would, like a father, tell us when we were at fault as well. It was so liberating. Sometimes I wept at the freshness of it all.

Every so often some of us would talk over what we were really hearing Jesus say and what we understood by it. I don't think we saw the scale of the storm we were running into, but we saw the huge generosity at the heart of his message. One of us said it was like a warm wind blowing from the future. (It might have been Andrew—I sometimes caught him looking out wistfully in the direction of the Sea of Galilee—once a fisherman always a fisherman . . .) and that warm wind was bringing love, hope, justice, forgiveness, peace, a world characterized by gratitude and joy. It was heady stuff.

So if this was what God was wanting for us, of course he would respond to our prayers. The point of Jesus' story of the unpleasant judge lies in the phrase 'how much more', which Jesus often used. God is always 'more', I was coming to realize. More in love, more in grace, more in beauty, more in forgiveness, more in justice. Just 'more'.

I could trust my life to this God. And to the man I trusted more than any other to take me to him.

> *I wonder what the importance of persistence in prayer really is, if God is not actually like the unjust judge who needs to be worn down?*
>
> *I wonder how you imagine Jesus thought up his parables? Did he prepare them all beforehand, ready for use, or think of them spontaneously, or adapt stories that were common in the culture—or what?*
>
> *I wonder what stories have been important to you in your own faith journey?*
>
> *I wonder what stories we might use in communicating our faith today?*

Saturday poem

―――――◆●◆―――――

'Welcome to the real world' by Godfrey Rust

I'm beginning to understand.
I saw a sign once
outside a church. It said
Are you really living
or just walking around
to save the expense of a funeral?

I didn't know
that Love is real life,
and everything else
just a more or less entertaining way
of dying.

And I didn't know
that Love is like nothing on earth.

Love isn't what you fall in.
It's what pulls you out
of what you fall in.

Love isn't a good feeling.
Love is doing good
when you're feeling bad.

Love means hanging in
when everyone else
shrugs their shoulders
and goes off to McDonalds.

Love means taking the knocks
and coming back
to try to make things better.

Saturday poem: 'Welcome to the real world'

Love hurts.
It's its way of telling you
that you're alive.

And the funny thing is that after all
Love does feel good.
People say Love is weak.
But Love is tougher than Hate.
Hating's easy.
Most of us have a gift for it.

But Love counts to ten
while Hate slams the door.
Love says *you*
where Hate says *me*.

Love is the strongest weapon
known to mankind.
Other weapons blow people up.
Only Love puts them back together again.

And everything that seems real,
that looks smart,
that feels good,
has a sell-by date.
But Love has no sell-by date.
Love is Long Life.
Love is the ultimate preservative.

I don't know too much about Love
but I know a man who does,
up there on the cross
loving us to death.

Love is the key
to the door of the place
he's prepared for you
in the kingdom of God.

If you're beginning to understand
then welcome to the real world.

Week 3

*I wonder how you would describe the real world in the light
of this poem?*

I wonder how Love has operated in your life?

*I wonder how you've experienced the cross as a sign and
source of Love?*

WEEK 4

———◆·●·◆———

Monday

———◆·●·◆———

Amazing grace: Luke 18.9–28

Jesus was smiling broadly. Peter was telling one of his tall stories, and Jesus had clearly been egging him on, poking fun at him gently. I loved it when he relaxed like that: the times when he was just a young man with his friends, chatting, laughing, and joking; the times when we chased local children through the fields, or stripped off and dived into the lake on a boiling hot day. He needed time off and some normality.

But it was another day, another crowd. Another opportunity to teach those golden stories to people eager to be lifted beyond their everyday struggles and given some hope and vision. I honestly don't know how he did it, how he met every new group with warmth and encouragement, or sometimes a warning, but always with a challenge, and nearly always with a new story. Of course some of them got repeated—why not? It's what every preacher does with his favorite stories. But each time they came out freshly minted and spoke straight to the heart.

It was a morning like many others. We'd been on the road to Jerusalem for a while now, never getting very far in a day because of all the people we met who wanted a piece of Jesus. We stopped for a drink in a village down toward Jericho, and a crowd gathered as usual. Jesus took a long drink, and then turned to the expectant faces, smiled, and said, 'Let me tell you a story.'

It was about two favorite characters in Jesus' stories, a Pharisee and a tax collector. They were stereotypes of course, but useful for making the points he wanted to get across, this time about the tax collector being the one who had God's favor rather than the religious leader. It was always the shock factor that I enjoyed, watching people's faces. I mean, years of conditioning would have led to the assumption that if anyone would be in God's good books it would be the faithful, dependable, disciplined, tithing Pharisee. He was the religious ideal, surely. On the other hand, the tax collector worked for a foreign government and took taxes from his own people, participating in a corrupt system. He was a traitor and religiously unclean, a thoroughly disreputable character. So it was crazy for the tax collector to be the one whom God commended.

But you could then see the shock turning to understanding as they recognized that the taxman was making no claims to worthiness; he was just presenting himself before God and throwing himself on God's mercy. There was honesty and humility in that, not the kind of 'see-how-good-I-am-You-owe-me-one' approach of the Pharisee. Of course! None of us can earn our way to God's blessing; it comes absolutely free as gift and grace to anyone who isn't full of their own goodness. Indeed grace is the word we often used later on when we looked back on Jesus' life—amazing grace.

And then, as if on cue, a group of mothers began to creep forward and bring their babies for Jesus to touch. And sadly I'm afraid this showed up how much we, the friends and companions of Jesus, still had to learn. I'm embarrassed to think of it, but right after this powerful story about grace, we denied it. We told the mothers to back off. I suppose in our minds

Jesus was doing man's work here and shouldn't be distracted with babies. We were going to Jerusalem and something very significant was going to happen there. We'd been told Herod was threatening to kill Jesus. Tensions were mounting. Serious things were afoot and Jesus shouldn't be wasting time and effort on these little babies.

How wrong could we be! Jesus pointed it out immediately. He loved children anyway, even these tiny ones who weren't yet five and ready to go to religious school (which they would if they were boys). But these babies were precisely an example of what he'd just been talking about with the tax collector. It's impossible to deserve the kingdom, to have a claim on it. It's an unconditional gift. Babies have no social status; they're just themselves. They can only receive. So it must be with us if we are to enter the kingdom. We can't march in; we have to be carried.

Twelve young men looked rather shame-faced.

As if to make the point even clearer, Jesus then got into a discussion with a wealthy young man who wanted to demonstrate his good intentions but wasn't able to let go of his many possessions. I suppose he had become so saturated in his material success he couldn't really let go and trust everything to God. He wanted to serve both God and that popular idol, mammon. 'Not on,' said Jesus, and the young man was clearly very downhearted. I think Jesus was genuinely sorry for him. It wasn't that money was wrong, just that everything had to come second to our allegiance to God.

I suppose James and I, and Peter and Andrew too, had an easier decision in some ways. Not that we were poor; our family fishing businesses were pretty well rewarded, but we didn't have as much to give up as the young man that day. But we were still so slow to 'get it'. That incident with the babies had shown us that rather too vividly. We may have heard the message from Jesus time and again and nodded in keen agreement, but it's a long distance from the head to the heart.

*I wonder what messages the young mothers took away
that day?*

*I wonder what the wealthy young man might have done
next?*

*I wonder whether that message of grace has really penetrated
our hearts too? Do we sometimes thank God we aren't
like that Pharisee?*

I wonder how we might know that we've 'got it' at last?

Tuesday

What do you see? Luke 18.31–43

Before we carried on from our mid-morning stop with all that teaching, the babies, the wealthy young man, and so on, Jesus wanted a quiet word with us. It felt very special that he would take us into his confidence like that. We were just a bunch of young lads from the north country, but Jesus had chosen us to be his companions—us! So we asked the crowd to give us some space and went into a huddle under a nearby tree.

But I'm sorry to say, Jesus really confused us. He said what he'd intimated a few times before, but which this time he really spelt out. We were going up to Jerusalem where he would be handed over to the foreigners, tortured, killed—and then 'rise again'. Well, it was all so way out. Yes, there were some worrying signs here and there, Herod's threats for instance, but Jesus was so popular. We saw it everywhere. He was giving people hope. They left him with a light in their eye, as if they were suddenly looking at life in a new way. There might be a few of those tussles with the religious authorities again, but surely torture and death weren't on the menu. And as for the suggestion that he would 'rise again', what on earth did that mean? Dead is dead, and he wasn't going to die anyway.

So we tried to look serious, as if we understood and sympathized, but we wandered off muttering quietly to one another, 'What was all that about?'

We picked up our bags and set off again. People smiled and thanked us as we left. Some of the less inhibited ran up to Jesus and stroked him, as if something magical might rub off. And we knew that sometimes it did!

As we got nearer to Jericho, we noticed that the pace was picking up. It seemed as if Jesus felt we were getting close and he wanted to get on with it, whatever 'it' was. Jesus was ten years older than some of us, but he was as fit as anyone and he led us down the track with steady purpose and what seemed like steely determination. It was both magnificent and scary.

But as we came near to the ancient city of Jericho, we soon came to a stop. I've always liked Jericho. They call it the oldest city on earth. Certainly we Jews have lived here for a very long time, deep down in that burning cauldron where nothing would grow if it wasn't for the spring that's poured out its water so gloriously for so long. Jericho is a perfect stopping place the night before you start that hard, dangerous slog up to Jerusalem. We were going to do just that.

But as we entered the city, there was a blind man at the side of the road. That was where they usually gathered so as not to get in the way but also so that they could beg more openly from the travelers who were arriving in the city. (I call it a city even though there were only a few hundred people and a couple of palaces—but it was an oasis of green in a harsh yellow landscape.) Anyway, here he was, this blind beggar, and he soon learned from those around him who we were—or who Jesus was. He began shouting, 'Jesus, Son of David, your mercy, please.' Now I realized straight away that this might be difficult for Jesus. To be associated with our great King David would have suggested that, deep down, Jesus was trying to be a powerful military figure intending to drive foreigners out of our land, and the message we heard so often from Jesus was that this wasn't his way. He came in peace. His weapons were love and forgiveness, not slingshot and sword. What the blind man was saying wasn't a message Jesus wanted to get around.

So I wasn't surprised that Jesus stopped and asked for the man to be brought forward so that they could meet properly. In any case, he had a special thing about blindness and often used that image in his teaching. He'd said right at the start when we were in the synagogue in Capernaum and he'd been handed the scroll to read, that he'd come to bring good news to the poor, freedom to captives, and recovery of sight to the blind. Nevertheless, I was a bit taken aback when I heard what Jesus said next. He looked at this poor disheveled figure standing before him in pathetic clothes, with eyes that wandered about sightlessly, and he said, 'What do you want me to do for you?' Come on, Jesus! Isn't that a bit obvious? But now I think he was saying, 'OK, here you are, but are you prepared to *own* your deepest need, to say it, and to take the consequences of getting your sight back? You won't be able to sit here and beg. You'll have to work for a living. You'll have to be a responsible citizen and help others. *What do you want me to do for you*?'

But this was the chance of a lifetime for the blind beggar. He wasn't going to back off to smaller things. He turned his face to Jesus. 'Lord, let me see again,' he said bravely. And Jesus did. He did as we'd seen him do so many times. It always brought tears to my own eyes. But Jesus reminded him straight off that it had been his bold faith that had made the difference. In other words, 'Don't forget what faith in God can do. Don't run off and ignore the One who's given you your life back.'

He certainly didn't run off. He stayed with us, wanting to keep close to Jesus, wanting to thank God and to tell others.

Just what Jesus would have hoped for, in fact.

> *I wonder what the disciples would have done with those*
> *   predictions of death and resurrection? Worried about*
> *   them? Disbelieved them? Ignored them?*
> *I wonder what might have happened to the blind man?*
> *I wonder what we don't really 'see' in our faith?*
> *I wonder what we, as a society, don't really 'see'?*

Wednesday

Little man, big tree: Luke 19.1–10

We spent the night on the edge of the town and set off next morning for the last fifteen miles of stiff walking up to Jerusalem. The sun was on our backs, the salty shore of the Dead Sea away to our left, and the mountains up ahead. As we continued into Jericho, more and more people came out to meet us. The man who'd just got his sight back seemed to have been a well-known character locally, so they were intrigued to see him (he was still with us), but mainly they wanted to see Jesus. Word got around fast in these villages, and Jesus was quite a celebrity now. We rather enjoyed it, basking in the reflected fame, accepting little gifts, smiling at the girls. If this is what it would be like in Jerusalem, we were in for a good time.

We wanted to walk right through the town and get on to the mountain road, but near the center, where the crowds were thickest, Jesus suddenly stopped. He'd spotted someone up a tree, a mulberry fig I think—I'm not very good on trees. Why Jesus noticed this one man when there were so many others was one of those mysteries I never understood. He just had a sense for these things. Anyway, he stood at the bottom of this tree, looked up and said, 'Zacchaeus, come on down, I want to visit your house.' Now, first, how did he know his name, and second, why on earth did he want to do a house call when we had to get on to Jerusalem by nightfall? We certainly didn't want to be on that dangerous road after dark.

It turned out that Zacchaeus was another well-known Jericho character, but for all the wrong reasons. He was the boss of a group of tax collectors, who operated for the hated Romans by collecting tolls on the movement of our farm produce and the other goods we made. And of course they took a rake-off of their own as well. They say money talks, but with these tax collectors it seemed that money shouted. It certainly made more noise than honesty and respect. These people were usually rich, smug, and despised. But Jesus had met enough of them to know that there was a deep sickness in most of them, something he could heal.

I have to tell you, it was a comical sight, seeing this little man slipping and sliding out of the tree as he hurried down to meet Jesus. I never asked him why he'd set aside his tattered dignity to climb a tree and see a traveling preacher. Maybe he was already feeling the tug of contrition. Maybe the split in his personality was becoming too wide to tolerate. Anyway, down he slithered and in a flustered voice said he would be honored if Jesus came to his house for a little refreshment before he moved on. The crowd was clearly unhappy and, I have to say, we were a bit frustrated too. As far as the crowd was concerned, it was bizarre to go and eat with a miserable little tax collector, giving him the kudos that went with sharing a meal when everyone knew that sinners couldn't be accepted into table fellowship. And anyway, as far as we were concerned, we still had a hard day's uphill trek and wanted to be on our way.

Reluctantly we trooped off to Zacchaeus's place. The twelve of us felt like country cousins as we looked around in amazement at the rich furnishings, the sumptuous wall hangings, and the delicious sweetmeats the servants conjured up. Soon, though, we realized that Jesus and Zacchaeus were already deep in conversation. I caught up with it just in time to hear Zacchaeus blurt out that he wanted to give half his possessions to the poor and to pay back four times over the people he'd cheated. We looked around at this beautiful house; I think Judas was doing some mental sums. If he really meant what he'd said about paying victims back, that was quite a promise; he would be in seriously reduced circumstances. He'd have to change his lifestyle big time. In any case, giving away half his possessions was far beyond the law's requirement of a tenth, and offering fourfold recompense was at the extreme end of what was required in restitution for a crime. But this was the effect Jesus had on people. They discovered depths of generosity they didn't know they had.

Jesus looked at him in that unnerving way he had, which seemed to penetrate right into your soul. 'Zacchaeus,' he said, 'I knew you had it in you. It's not just me who's come to your house today; it's salvation that's come to your house. You're back in the fold where you belong, a child of Abraham.' Zacchaeus beamed. Jesus beamed. We all beamed. And Jesus said, 'You know, this is really what I came for. I came to search out those who've got themselves lost and to help them back on the right road. Which reminds me, we must get back onto our own road. We've got a lot to do.'

How terribly true that was.

> *I wonder how it was for Zacchaeus, staying on and living*
> *   in Jericho after Jesus left?*
> *I wonder how we could echo Jesus in spotting people in need?*
> *I wonder if you've ever seen a significant change of heart*
> *   result from someone encountering Jesus?*
> *I wonder what difference encountering Jesus has had on you?*

Thursday

———•◆•———

The ten pounds: Luke 19.11–27

There were so many different sides to Jesus. I don't mean that in a negative way, that you didn't know if you could trust him; of course you could, with your life (which many of our small band actually had to do eventually of course). I mean that he was so full of life that he seemed to exhibit in himself what it was to be a real human being. It's hard to explain. I'd seen him in a huge variety of settings, public and private, relaxed and under pressure, adored and disliked, and I can honestly say I never saw him get it wrong. That doesn't mean he didn't get cross when someone was particularly obtuse, or yell when he hit his thumb with a hammer, but it does mean that his response to every situation seemed somehow not just appropriate (that's such a bland word) but the *correct* one, the *right* one in those circumstances.

Anyway, there was this other time when at first I thought he'd blown it and actually got it wrong. He was telling another story and, as so often, it was about someone going off to a far country and leaving his servants to look after things. No problem: the person going off equals Jesus, the servants equal us. The servants were given some money to use properly while he was away, and this equaled our responsibility to look after Israel's life and faith profitably. The trouble was the main figure was a really distasteful character, a nobleman going off to be made a king, who then comes back and lays into one of his servants because he's tried to preserve what he's been entrusted with. And the king accepts the servant's description of him that he's a harsh man with an eye for the main chance.

You can see why I thought Jesus had blown it. Why put forward such an image of himself? Why suggest that he was prepared to be so brutal? I didn't get it. But after a while I began to see. I talked it over with James and Peter, as usual, and we pieced it together. James is wise, always has been. Peter's more instinctive, but often spot on. So we did what Jesus always wanted us to do of course, to worry away at his stories and get to the deeper meaning that might begin to change us. So what follows is where we got to—but I don't claim we've understood this story at all thoroughly.

First let me paint in a bit of local color. When Herod the Tyrant died (sorry if that's a bit blunt, but he was terrible), his older son Archelaus wanted to carry on where he left off, at least inasmuch as being king like his father. So he went off to Rome to be confirmed in that role. He was so despised, however, that a delegation of Judeans followed him to object, and he came back not as king but just as 'ruler' over Judea, and that position itself lasted only for a short time. So we reckoned Jesus was saying that he himself was coming to Judea as the real king, not the harsh taskmaster but the generous, gracious, and just king everyone wanted.

In other words it was another of Jesus' contrasts: 'how much more' would the true king do the right thing in the right way. I wonder if you remember how I told you Jesus' story about a dishonest land manager being praised by his master, and then later another story about a judge who eventually, reluctantly, got up to give someone some bread for a late-night visitor? In both cases Jesus was using rather disreputable characters to draw the contrast with who he was and what he was trying to do. It was a risky feature of Jesus' storytelling but, consequently, all the more effective.

But here in this story about the ten pounds (a mina, by the way, and worth about three months' wages for a laborer) he was also being absolutely straight with us, and it was a very tough message. He was saying if we didn't respond to the invitation and the demands of the kingdom that he was announcing, we were in deep water. If we didn't use the opportunity (the ten mina), we had only ourselves to blame when judgment came upon us. To refuse the offer was to refuse God and that way led to disaster. It was a message we came to understand much more vividly as we went through that dark week in Jerusalem. We weren't playing religious games. To stick with the world's ways of self-interest, power-seeking, greed, vengeance, and so on was to bring a judgment on ourselves, not because God was capricious but simply because there was nothing else left to use—the mina had been wrapped up in a piece of cloth unused.

In the heady days after Jesus had left us and we were basking in the reality of his Spirit, James and I often remembered this story. Yes, the prince had left to claim his throne, but he would return and ask if we'd used his gift well, if the joy of the kingdom had flooded the world, and if we'd established the principles of peace and justice in every land. It was a tall order, but this was a tall kingdom.

Now here I am, thinking back on all these things that have happened over the years. Sometimes I think we're doing quite well and the green shoots of the kingdom are springing up everywhere. And sometimes I think human nature is simply too resistant and we'll never get there. But I guess that's ultimately for God to sort out. As I see it, our job is just to be faithful. As Jesus often said, just keep putting the kingdom of God first.

That's the task I take on afresh every day.

I wonder how confused the disciples might have been by some of these parables?

I wonder how we hold together in our picture of Jesus his compassion and attractiveness along with his robust teaching and tough warnings?

I wonder whether we should respond to our unproductiveness in terms of the kingdom with renewed effort, guilt, self-forgiveness, or what?

I wonder what we learn from all this about how we should speak to the modern world? How should we talk about God?

Friday

Olives and tears: Luke 19.28–44

That last fifteen miles climbing up to Jerusalem was always a struggle. And you were keeping an eye out for robbers too, though a group of our size was safer than most. It was hot, and the route was winding and dusty, but we were young and eager to get there, to reach the goal of our long journey. There wasn't much talking, because we were too focused on our individual effort, and some of us had a really hard time of it, like Matthew, who'd spent too many years sitting at a tax collector's booth and eating too well in the evenings. But finally we made it. We went past Bethany and Bethphage, villages that were familiar because our friends Mary, Martha, and Lazarus lived there, but we didn't stop this time. We pushed on that little bit more and emerged at the top of the Mount of Olives, looking down with wonder again on the holy city laid out before us, the Temple gleaming in the sun, the great walls daring anyone to challenge the city's strength and smugness. It was always exciting to get to this point, to look over the city that held our memories and dreams as a nation, and to ponder the religious and political power that resided there and the emotions that surged back and forth through its crowded streets.

We were getting our breath back, each lost in his own thoughts, when Jesus suddenly took command. He'd obviously planned the next bit because he sent two of us to pick up a young colt from the villages just behind us. They were accosted by two of the locals, but when they said who wanted it, it was clear all was well. And then we set off, Jesus on the young donkey, and us—well, somehow we knew what to do. Peter started it. This was a royal event, the arrival of a king, so it was clear we should lay cloaks on the ground before the king and sing psalms about the king who was coming in the name of the Lord. People began to come up from the city and down from the villages, and soon everyone was getting into the spirit of the occasion. 'Blessed is the king who comes in the name of the Lord.' It felt as if we really were welcome, that our growing unease on the journey had been misplaced. All would be well.

But I had the strangest, dream-like moment in the middle of it all. It felt as though I was standing apart from what was happening and looking on both at this little procession coming from the east, from Jericho, and another great procession coming from the west, from Caesarea. On the west side was Pilate, riding in on his huge war horse to remind Jerusalem who was boss at one of our main festivals. On the east side was a young preacher riding in on a lowly donkey to bring peace to our land. On the one side was cruelty and oppression; on the other, forgiveness, and freedom. On one side unrestrained power; on the other unrestrained love. It was a giddy contrast, but it planted a picture in my mind that became stronger every day through that momentous week. Here was a stark choice, even a mighty battle, being laid out before us.

I snapped back into the present. Some Pharisees had appeared from the city and were clearly concerned about the psalms of praise we were singing. Whether they were worried about our safety, like those who had warned us Herod was out to kill Jesus, or concerned that these royal associations would bring Rome crashing down on everyone, I don't know, but I do know that Jesus gave a robust response to the effect that if we were silent the very stones beneath us would take up the song and shout aloud. It was a lovely picture. This was Jesus' moment, and all Creation was sharing it.

Then suddenly Jesus stopped. We'd come to another particular viewpoint over the city and I could see that Jesus was in tears. It stopped us all in our tracks—the singing died on our lips. I went closer to put a hand on his arm in silent sympathy, and I heard him murmuring in real distress. 'If only you had recognized the offer of peace . . . if only . . . if only . . . But you can't see it! And the consequences . . .' I moved away. I was intruding on a desperately personal moment. I think Jesus was suddenly overcome with the sadness of what this great city and its chosen people had persisted in doing with the prophets and which he feared it was going to do again now. They were offered the way of peace but always rejected the offer and chose the way of war. They were going to play right into the oppressors' hands, as they had done so often with the Babylonians, the Seleucids, the Romans. The result was always exile and destruction, and Jesus knew it. If only they could recognize God's moment . . .

Jesus pulled himself together, and we continued the last few hundred yards to the Kidron valley and the Garden they called Gethsemane. But we walked silently now. This was serious business. Jesus' eyes told a different story from the one they had told at the start.

But in those eyes, too, there was steel.

I wonder how much Jesus had orchestrated parts of this week?

I wonder what the local crowds thought when this Jesus came in on a donkey and his friends sang these royal psalms and laid cloaks before him?

I wonder if there was anything Jesus' friends could have said to him when he was in tears?

I wonder what you think and feel about the Jerusalem of today?

Saturday poem

'Transcendence' by Veronica Popescu

Not for three months, let alone nine
could Mary conceal His presence—
nor was Joseph kept in the dark
before His eruption like the morning star
at midnight breaking in winter—
He dazzled both shepherds and wisemen:
we twelve were all blinded—three years—
till flesh failed to veil Him, even from us,
in a calm stilled sea, and on one mountain top.
How then could we conspire to cover Him
with heavy human robes—bury Him
in puny feudal powers? Him,
whose setting the sun mourned,
whose light Death could not extinguish?
He burst out of that grave, propelled
by resurrection—casting us all before Him
by the blaze of his uprising.

I wonder which phrases most caught your attention?
I wonder what the poet meant by 'bury him in puny feudal powers'?
I wonder what difference the resurrection makes to your own life?
I wonder what have been your most compelling experiences of transcendence?

WEEK 5

———◆•◆———

Monday

———◆•◆———

The Temple: Luke 19.45–48

It was only a short walk from Gethsemane up the steep hill to the famous Temple. What a building that was, standing proud and magnificent in the sun, shining with self-confidence. Herod had done an amazing job restoring it with all the grandeur it deserved. After all, it contained the sacred text of the Torah, the law, which our people had guarded through thick and thin from Moses onward. People had loved this sacred Law, fought for it, died for it. It was kept in the Ark in the holy of holies, opened only once a year on the Day of Atonement. They said it had incredible power, and if you handled it wrongly, you would die.

The Temple was a daunting place for the thirteen of us to enter, dusty working men from the north country. A phrase from the Psalms kept coming into my mind, 'I was glad when they said to me, let us go to the house of the Lord. My feet are standing within your gates, O Jerusalem.' This was the heart of the nation, our identity, the place of sacrifice and forgiveness—indeed, the very place of God's presence. It felt as if we were steeped in holiness and raw power. We went in and stood in the middle of the outer court as self-important priests pushed past us, and poor pilgrims stood around looking lost, and sad-looking sheep in pens awaited their fate.

Then suddenly I heard a crash. Jesus had gone berserk and was turning over tables and chasing out the locals who were changing money and selling animals for sacrifice. It was chaotic, but before describing what happened, a bit of background might help. The Temple tax had to be paid in silver, but Rome didn't allow us Jews to mint silver coins, so we had to get them from elsewhere, from Tyre. Shekels from Tyre were particularly pure, and they weren't stamped with the hated image of Roman emperors. On the other hand, they had images of an eagle on one side and the pagan god Melkart on the other, so, as you can imagine, that didn't go down well with Jesus. Then there were the people selling animals. They were making a packet from overcharging poor pilgrims who had to buy animals for sacrifice. So the whole commercial enterprise in the Temple was corrupt. It stank.

And now Jesus was going around creating mayhem and shouting that God said his house would be a house of prayer, not a den of robbers. It was strong stuff. I'd never seen Jesus so angry and determined: tables and chairs were all over the place, money scattered on the floor, pigeons escaping while the going was good. When things had calmed down later that evening, someone said it seemed as if Jesus was acting out the prophecies of Isaiah and Jeremiah about the abuse of the sacrificial system in the Temple, but at the time it just seemed as if Jesus had lost it. I couldn't decide whether to move in and try to take Jesus away, or to keep clear and avoid getting hurt!

But I think there might have been an even deeper message in this extraordinary incident, which the Temple authorities probably latched onto as well, and that was about the whole place of the Temple in our life as a nation. Put simply, it had gotten too big for itself. It couldn't contain God (Solomon had always said that), but it kind of imagined it could. So the priests had assumed more authority than they could handle, and the building had almost taken over the significance of the God it served. It had lost its way, and God's judgment was inevitable. And, to be fair, Jesus had warned about this earlier in the day when he'd wept over the city and said that it would be crushed to the ground and not one stone would be left standing on another. And here he was, acting it out.

Eventually, I plucked up courage and guided Jesus out, who was breathing heavily, but not before I'd seen the chief priests and their scribes gathered in a huddle by the gate to the inner courts, talking earnestly. It looked dangerous to me, but then, when someone comes into your house and turns it upside down, any of us might get mad. If Jesus had wanted to make a public announcement of his arrival in Jerusalem, he couldn't have done it any more effectively. But I couldn't help wondering if he was also saying that this Temple really belonged to him and it was his duty to clear it up. When he said '*My* house' did he mean just that, and that he wanted it back?

As we had supper that evening back in Bethany, Jesus began to talk in more measured tones about needing to 'purify' the Temple because he wanted to go there during the week and teach. I asked him why he hadn't warned us of what he planned to do. He smiled sheepishly and said that if he had, we'd have tried to stop him. Too true! But it felt somehow as if the Temple now acknowledged him, the leaders were going to reject him, and the people would be held spellbound by him, as they always were.

But as for me, a shiver went down my spine.

> *I wonder when Jesus might have decided he would go into the Temple and turn it upside down?*
> *I wonder if Jesus wanted to make a point, to announce his arrival and to stir things up—or was he just angry?*
> *I wonder what there is about our religious establishment that annoys you?*
> *I wonder what we can do about it?*

Tuesday

Controversy: Luke 20.1–19

We woke late the next day, and as usual Jesus was outside praying. He never missed. He said it was as necessary to him as breathing. Sometimes I wondered where he got his extraordinary energy and wisdom from, and this was it. He spent time with the one he called Abba. And he certainly needed wisdom that day.

After we'd eaten a good breakfast together, he asked just a few of us to come with him to the Temple. I don't think he wanted to be as noticeable today, and after yesterday, some of us agreed with him. So in we went. Jesus was in good humor. He seemed relieved somehow; perhaps because we'd gotten here at last after so many days of walking, and now he could get on with what he'd come to do—to present his teaching to the people and the powers that be in Jerusalem and see how they responded. Galilee loved him, for the most part, but what would it be like in Jerusalem? So we went to the outer court of the Temple and set ourselves up under the colonnades, and Jesus began speaking. He didn't teach anything different from what he had taught in Galilee. It was the good news of God's kingdom of justice and joy, breaking in right now and coming to fulfilment quite soon. It was about God's exciting love for his people, and his desire to give everyone a new start in his kingdom of peace and freedom, where everyone was welcome.

It didn't take long for yesterday's suspicious group of chief priests, scribes, and elders to gather nearby. It seemed as if they'd been waiting for us. One of them, a tall man with a faint air of superiority, came over and asked Jesus by what authority he did these things. I supposed he meant the drama in the Temple the day before, but I think he was also asking where Jesus got the authority to teach in this place that so clearly belonged to the clergy. In the synagogues around the country you could have laypeople participating in leading worship and sometimes you could even invite them to speak to the assembly; but not in the Temple—this was priest country. From their point of view I suppose it was a fair question.

I'm sure you know Jesus' answer, which was about his cousin John the Baptizer: 'Where did John get his authority from?' It wasn't actually a trick question, as some felt it was. If they recognized John's authenticity as a messenger, they would recognize Jesus too, because it was at John's baptism of Jesus that the master's authenticity as God's chosen one had been revealed in a voice many people heard as he came out of the water. But, on the other hand, if John wasn't a true prophet, then Jesus was just a dreamer after all. So they ducked the question. Jesus realized they weren't going to be honest and said that he, therefore, didn't see the point of answering their original question either. So nothing was resolved.

Then Jesus turned back to the people who'd been listening to this discussion and began telling them a story about a man with a vineyard, some unpleasant tenants, and a succession of slaves sent to the tenants by the owner to ask for his share of the produce. The religious leaders stood there listening, stony-faced, but even they couldn't have known what was coming next. When the slaves were beaten up by the tenants, the land-owner finally sent his son, believing they wouldn't dare mistreat him, but they actually killed him, which finally brought down the anger of the landowner on them and the vineyard was given to others. The parallel couldn't have been more obvious: owner, God; tenants, Israel; slaves, the prophets. Which just left me anxious about the son, of course. Did he mean what I feared he meant?

But Jesus had moved on to another image now: a stone, rejected by the builders as not fitting in with the rest of the stones they were using in their construction work, but which turned out in the end to be the very stone they needed for a particular vital corner. Again, it wasn't hard for any of us to get the message. But it wasn't going to be popular with our little band of clerics. They stalked off, trying to maintain their dignity.

We might have guessed—a few minutes later another bunch turned up, obviously sent by the chief priests, and they tried a different approach, acting all smarmy, saying they knew Jesus was right in what he said and taught the true way of God, and could he help them with a little problem they had? Should they pay taxes to the emperor or not? (Jesus looked over at the three or four disciples who were there, and I could have sworn I saw a wink.) The question was a nasty little ploy, but Jesus quickly turned it upside down. He got them to produce a denarius—which they shouldn't have had anyway because it had on it the blasphemous image of Tiberius Caesar and an inscription that proclaimed him to be son of God. Then Jesus went for the kill. He said, fine, that's Caesar on the coin, so give him what he deserves (a double meaning if ever there was one!), but give *God* what *he* deserves—which they were singularly failing to do in the way they were corrupting the Temple. The coin bears the image of Caesar, so it belongs to him; but we bear the image of God, so we belong to God, as does everything about us. In effect he was saying give your money to Caesar but yourself to God.

I have to say, it was very gratifying. But equally clearly, Jesus was not winning any friends in this place, the heart of the system he had come to challenge.

I began to realize it could only end in tears.

I wonder if Jesus was deliberately winding them up?

I wonder if the disciples grasped the predictions (as in the parable) of his death?

I wonder what in our day we think belongs to Caesar and what belongs to God?

I wonder how much of your life belongs to God?

Wednesday

Resurrection: Luke 20.27–47

I honestly can't remember where all of us got to during those confrontational days in the Temple. I know we always made sure there were sufficient of us to support Jesus, to go and get water and food, to run errands, get supplies for the evening meal, and so on, but I suppose some of us had family in the city and went off to see them. Some may have gone for a wander through the throbbing streets, full of color and smells and noise, so different from the calm of Galilee. Our little band, so tight-knit on our journey, was now breaking up. I hoped we weren't losing our focus and being seduced by the city; Jesus certainly couldn't lose his concentration.

They seemed to come in waves. Next up were some Sadducees with one of their special trick questions. We'd just had some lunch, sitting there under the colonnades out of the sun, and we might actually have been nodding off just a little, when a group of these upper-crust religious leaders came straight up and shot a question at Jesus, clearly with the intention of wrong-footing him.

It's worth knowing who this lot were. Sadducees were from the priestly class, usually wealthy, and very conservative. They recognized only the five books of the Pentateuch as authoritative and therefore any concept of resurrection was obviously unacceptable, and that led to heated debates with the Pharisees, who not only recognized the prophets and other writings as scriptural but also accepted the oral tradition from Moses, which was where the ideas about resurrection mostly came from. So these Sadducees weren't coming to Jesus with a genuine inquiry;

they knew what they believed about their question and just wanted to bait Jesus and embarrass him.

They had a range of trick questions and the one Jesus got was about a woman who married seven brothers one after the other, the question being whose wife she would be in the resurrection (so called). Jesus stood up and looked coolly at them for a while. He was weighing them up, but you could see that his level gaze was having a disconcerting effect on them. Then he seemed to decide which approach to take. In fact, he took two. First, he said, it will all be different in the age to come. Death will be finished, and there won't be any need to keep a family line going, so the question is irrelevant. Those who are raised will be like angels in the sense that they'll be children of the resurrection, with resurrection bodies, not ones like ours. And second (Jesus took them to their own ground, the five books of Moses), he said they must have noticed that Moses wrote of the Lord being the God of Abraham, Isaac, and Jacob, and as he is God of the living, not the dead, our famous forefathers must be alive in God too.

The Sadducees looked bewildered, though their aristocratic bearing helped them disguise it to some extent. But the scribes who had hung around seemed jubilant. They must have been scribes of the Pharisees, because they congratulated Jesus warmly on his answer. Meanwhile the Sadducees, with a disdainful swirl of expensive robes, turned and left. Jesus smiled.

Then he had another idea. There was quite a crowd now, enjoying the various debates and seeing their usually imperious leaders baffled by this quick-witted and engaging preacher. Jesus had been watching the retreating Sadducees, and then he turned back to these good people and fixed his clear, searching gaze on them. I think he must have been in a particular discussion recently, one I didn't recognize, because he referred to people saying that the Messiah is David's son. 'How can they say that?' he asked. I don't think he actually said it was from Psalm 110 (I was proud I recognized it), but he certainly quoted it. 'The Lord said to my Lord, "Sit at my right hand, until I make your enemies your footstool".' 'So', said Jesus, 'if David, the author of the psalm, calls him Lord, how can he be his son as well?'

It sounded a bit convoluted, but actually it was an important point. Jesus was saying to his listeners that most people's idea of the Messiah was too narrow. The Messiah will be David's Lord, not David's son, and he will be sharing the very throne of God. This wasn't just a human king who would fight their battles and rule well; this was one who would be in some way the embodiment of God himself.

The big question I was left with was almost too much to cope with. My head burst with the implications. Was Jesus claiming to be this Messiah, this immense figure, chosen not just in the sense I'd so far believed, as a special teacher with a unique place in the line of the prophets, but somehow as an embodiment of God right here among us now? I stood back and did a double take. This was the young leader I was thrilled to call my friend: he stood the same height as me, with the same color eyes; we'd fished together, eaten together, arm-wrestled; I'd seen him devour a plate of fish and bread faster than a hungry slave; I'd seen him laid out on the beach exhausted after a hard day; I'd seen him frustrated when he couldn't sew a tear in his clothes properly. How could this man, sparkling and fascinating as he was, be the Messiah?

It was too much to take in as I watched my friend sitting and talking with another crowd of pilgrims who'd just arrived for the festival. I didn't even feel I could voice the crazy idea with James, my wise brother. It seemed so wild. It was a question that would have to wait for another day.

> *I wonder if Jesus was clear on what he meant by the resurrection?*
> *I wonder how Jesus thought of himself in relation to the Messiah?*
> *I wonder what you imagine resurrection to mean?*
> *I wonder how you would justify your belief in the resurrection of the dead to those who don't have that belief?*

Thursday

Lessons from a widow: Luke 21.1–4

It had been a very demanding day. These controversial debates with powerful groups of religious officials had left us pretty drained. Peter, James, and I had really only been minders, but even we were tired. We tried to watch what was going on, to chat to people and see how they were responding to what Jesus was saying. Jesus would sometimes ask us at the end of the day what we'd heard or what we thought people were making of it all, or who people thought he was. (Once when we were away on retreat, he put us on the spot by asking not only 'Who are people saying that I am?' but also 'Who do *you* say that I am?' We stumbled a bit there, most of us, though Peter had it all worked out and typically didn't hold back.)

Anyway we'd stayed there, or thereabouts, with Jesus all day, though sometimes we'd slipped off for a drink at the fountain or to get Jesus some bread and hummus from a street seller. But we were all ready for a quiet evening—if such a thing were ever possible with such a lively group of Jesus' friends and followers. With thirteen young men taken from the land, from fishing boats, from building sites and all sorts of active lives, there always seemed to be some practical joke or play-fight, some energetic game or test of skill going on. But we all wanted to be off duty in the evenings if we could, so those of us who'd been with Jesus in the Temple were glad to start packing up and getting ready to return to the Mount of Olives.

But just then Jesus noticed what was going on at the treasury, where people made their gifts to the Temple and its work. He suddenly became intrigued, so we all put down whatever we were carrying and watched. We saw some obviously wealthy people, dressed in ornate robes, walk up proudly and confidently and place what were clearly considerable sums of money in the collection box. Am I imagining it or did they slow up when they were actually putting the money in the box and make a bit of a public show of it?

And then, even as we watched, we saw a woman, not very old, dressed in widow's clothes and with two small children, hovering around the treasury, waiting for her opportunity. She seemed to be nearly pushed over once or twice by those big, wealthy men I referred to. She scuttled out of their way, dragging her little ones along behind her. One of them was getting a little fractious; the other was in a dream. And then a gap appeared and the widow made a run for it, pulling what seemed to be just two small coins out of her pocket and quickly dropping them in the box. She stood for a moment, seeming somewhat dumbfounded at what she'd done, and then they hurried off.

Jesus was clearly moved by what we'd seen. Instinctively he seemed to know that while the wealthy had been generous, this widow had been sacrificial. The test was, he said, what was left after the gift had been made, and in his judgment, she had given everything and had nothing left. In a way I was amazed at such sacrifice and in a way I was shocked. How were those little ones to be fed if she'd given everything away? Wasn't she being irresponsible? But perhaps she simply had to demonstrate how much she loved and trusted God, knowing that he would sustain their family as he always did because that was the way they had to live, having so little.

I genuinely didn't know what to think about that. It troubled me, partly because I doubted I could ever come close to that kind of complete handing over of everything I had, and partly because I worried about that family's well-being and whether they had enough food in the house even tonight. I really hoped she came from a wider community, where they all supported one another and what she couldn't contribute in money she could offer in other ways. But that day she had offered the four of us who watched her give her last two copper coins a lesson in sacrifice and trust that would stay with me for a long time.

Or it would have done if other dark events hadn't been about to shatter my world.

> *I wonder what the disciples actually did when Jesus was about his business of teaching and healing?*
>
> *I wonder what was happening at this time to the disciples' understanding of who Jesus was?*
>
> *I wonder what you make of a mother giving away all she had to live on?*
>
> *I wonder what guidelines we might use for our giving to charity?*

Friday

---◆●◆---

The end: Luke 21.5–38

There was a side to Jesus that was really tough. We saw a huge amount of his compassionate side of course; I'd never met anyone who was so completely committed to the well-being of others and who gave them such focused attention. I'd seen him laboring long into the night with crowds of sick people, praying and healing. I'd seen him weeping when the emotional burden of his ministry became too great. But there was a steel core to him as well as this compassionate side. I used to talk to my parents, when I first met him, about this builder-carpenter from Nazareth who could charm the birds off the trees but who also spoke the truth in a way that made my brain burn. He would challenge people to be honest with themselves and with others. He would refuse easy answers to complex issues. He would tell people straight if he thought they were being false to their faith or ripping off the poor.

So I suppose it was no surprise that another strand to the teaching he did in the Temple that week was about the dire future facing Jerusalem and the Temple itself. There were three dark themes that I remember: the persecution that his followers faced, the destruction (no less) of the Temple, and the mysterious return of the Son of Man. I'll try and explain what he said and what we, his friends and followers, took him to mean.

He pulled no punches about persecution. He said we'd be arrested, put on trial, and find ourselves in prison. He even warned us that our own families would betray us in some cases. But he also said that this would give us an opportunity to witness to our faith. ('Thanks a lot!' said James quietly.) He said we shouldn't worry about working out complex arguments for our defense because he himself would give us words and wisdom that couldn't be gainsaid—though quite how he could do this for all of us he failed to mention.

Then he raised the stakes even higher. He said the Temple and the great city itself were doomed. Now remember where he was saying this. He was standing at the heart of this enormous edifice of the Temple, built over many decades with some of the largest stones ever moved on earth. It felt to us like the center of the universe, though I admit the Romans thought otherwise. And here was this young traveling preacher from Galilee saying it would all be destroyed, not one of those great stones left standing on another. At one level it seemed laughable. But we didn't laugh, because we knew the man who was saying these things. He said Jerusalem would be surrounded by armies (the Romans presumably), and we should then flee to the hills as fast as possible and take those with us that we could, especially those who were pregnant or had babies still at the breast. He said we ran the risk of being taken into captivity in foreign lands—another Exile—but Jerusalem itself would be flattened. It was a devastating vision. He didn't actually spell out that this was God's judgment on a city and a Temple that had fatally broken its covenant with him, but it was pretty well implied a number of times, and we all had that memory of the incident in the Temple a few days before, when he'd kind of 'acted out' that judgment.

But there was more to come. If we weren't already aghast at all this, Jesus had a third theme he spoke about, and that was the final end of the world as we knew it and the coming of the mysterious Son of Man on the clouds—an image taken from Daniel, I think. He spoke about all the forces of nature being disturbed—the sun, moon and stars, the seas, and even the heavens. He used the image of fig trees sprouting leaves, thus indicating the coming of summer. Similarly, he said, we could tell the Great Event was near because of all these happenings in nature. And yet, he said, and yet . . . we could stand tall when all this was under way because it would be a sign that our redemption was near. ('But what does that mean?' whispered James again.) Jesus said that all this would happen in this generation, so there was nowhere and no time to run. The only question so far as me and Thomas (who liked to get these things clear) were concerned was what was meant by 'this generation'? Was there a let-out clause there? In the meantime, said Jesus, we needed to be constantly on the alert and to be praying for strength to face the crisis when it came.

Well, you can imagine our nerves were somewhat shredded when we'd heard this teaching a time or two. We couldn't ignore it or wish it away, coming as it did from the man we trusted above all others. But equally it seemed so far-fetched as we stood among the magnificent buildings of the Temple, which looked well set for hundreds of years, and through which thousands of people were teeming all the time, oblivious to such extraordinary ideas.

Jesus was always exhausted when he'd finished this kind of preaching. It clearly gave him no pleasure, and it took a lot out of him. But he'd come with a prophetic message addressed to the heart of the nation's life, and he wouldn't compromise on that calling. And remember the steel core.

But that core would soon be put to much more terrible tests.

I wonder what the ordinary people made of Jesus' teaching on all this?

I wonder what you make of these 'apocalyptic' parts of the New Testament?

I wonder if you've ever been put to the test in having to witness to your faith?

I wonder what Jesus' 'second coming' means to us now?

Saturday poem

'Ballad of the Judas tree' by Ruth Etchells

In Hell there grew a Judas Tree
Where Judas hanged and died
Because he could not bear to see
His master crucified.

Our Lord descended into Hell
And found his Judas there
For ever hanging on the tree
Grown from his own despair.

So Jesus cut his Judas down
And took him in his arms
'It was for this I came' he said
'and not to do you harm.

'My Father gave me twelve good men
And all of them I kept
Though one betrayed and one denied
Some fled and others slept.

'In three days' time I must return
To make the others glad
But first I had to come to Hell
And share the death you had.

'My tree will grow in place of yours
Its roots lie here as well
There is no final victory
Without this soul from Hell.'

So when we all condemn him
As of every traitor worst
Remember that of all his men
Our Lord forgave him first.

> *I wonder if you are happy with Judas being forgiven first?*
> *I wonder what this 'harrowing of hell' might mean for us today?*
> *I wonder if you have ever been deeply forgiven or have forgiven deeply?*

WEEK 6

―――・●・―――

Monday

―――・●・―――

The last meal: Luke 22.1–38

Forgive me if I get a bit emotional at this point. We're entering the darkest time of my life, and I simply wasn't ready for it. You may say, surely we'd had enough warnings that these gathering clouds would have to burst over us sometime, but I hadn't realized quite what a disastrous storm it would be. I must have been living in a kind of romantic bubble in which Jesus could do anything and survive anything.

It began when, over breakfast, Jesus asked Peter and me to go into the city and prepare the Passover meal. It was the custom, if at all possible, for Jews to try and eat the Passover meal within the walls of the city, so what Jesus asked wasn't surprising. But what we weren't expecting was that, because Jesus knew the religious authorities were out to get him in some way or other, he'd arranged a clever method for us to find our way to the right room. It involved following a man carrying a jar of water (strange, because women do that) and a coded question to the owner of the house. Anyway we found it and spent a good deal of time setting the meal up. Peter was a bit clumsy at times, but we had a lot of good-hearted help from the women of the house and we knew this was a very important meal for Jesus—he often spoke about it—and we wanted to get it right. We had to get the bread, the wine, the herbs, the olives, cheese, spices, and of course the lamb, approved by a priest, with no broken bones and drained of blood, some of which was smeared on the door as a reminder of that first Passover in Egypt. There was a lot to do.

Well, we all gathered that evening, scrubbed up as well as we could, eager for a fine meal. It was great to be together again, having been rather dispersed during the previous few days, seeing friends and family around the city. And it was a memorable night—in too many ways. Jesus was in a strange mood, clearly enjoying being with his friends, but distracted as well, and sometimes I noticed him looking at Judas for rather a long time, as if trying to work something out. We were in high good humor to begin with, a group of friends gathered with our special friend, celebrating an eventful week of debate in which Jesus had clearly come out on top, and now gathered together for conversation over the most important meal of the year, marking as it did the escape of the Israelites from Egypt after the angel had 'passed over'.

After a while however, I began to sense a chill settling over the meal. It was odd; I couldn't put my finger on it. But then Jesus gave us bread and wine in a very memorable way, as if he wanted us to remember this all our lives. He changed the usual words of the Passover meal about the 'bread of affliction' and the 'cup of redemption' to bread that was his body and wine that was his blood. This was shocking, really shocking, because we Jews never, ever entertained the idea of drinking even an animal's blood, let alone a human's. Jesus talked about this sealing a new covenant, offering a new kind of freedom. It was perplexing. But I can tell you now, no meal with other followers of Jesus in future would ever be the same. No loaf now is just bread, no cup is just wine.

And then the evening hit a new low, because Jesus said that one of us would actually betray him. It was a horrendous idea. One of his faithful friends, whom he'd chosen after a night of prayer, one who had shared the highs and lows, been sent out to the villages on mission, who had eaten and prayed with him, and shared stories on the road. No. Impossible. Who on earth would do this?

But the pace of the evening was hotting up, even as the darkness gathered in our spirits. An argument flared up about who of us would be the greatest when Jesus had put everything right in his new kingdom, and Jesus had to sort us out and remind us that we were to serve each other, not lord it over each other. (Hadn't we got that yet?) But Jesus also said that the kingdom would indeed be ours because we had stood by him through everything.

And then another personal disaster: Jesus turned to Peter, good old big-hearted Peter, and told him Satan was after him and he would fail, but when he'd recovered he'd have a special role in encouraging the rest of us. Peter blurted out his loyalty, and then Jesus told him, to his face, that before the cock had crowed this very day he would have denied even knowing Jesus, not just once but three times. You can imagine what that did to Peter. It was crushing for a moment, but then he shook his big, shaggy head and you could see he didn't really believe it.

I looked around and noticed Judas wasn't there any longer.

The evening was going rapidly downhill. Jesus spoke in a low voice about what we, his friends, would need to do in the future. When we'd been out on mission in the past we'd not taken any money, bag, or spare sandals, but in future it would be different. We'd need them, because life would be much harder. We'd be on the run; there would be no hospitality and we'd have to rely on our own resources. Someone piped up that we already had two swords among us, but it was Jesus who now shook his head. 'No', he said. 'Enough of that kind of talk. It's time to go.'

And go we did, out into the night.

> *I wonder how you might have felt if you had been there that night?*
>
> *I wonder why Judas betrayed Jesus?*
>
> *I wonder if we betray Jesus in lesser ways?*
>
> *I wonder what sharing that bread and wine means to you personally now?*

Tuesday

Prayer and betrayal: Luke 22.39–53

That night it seemed that death was in the air. We set off from the room where we'd shared our momentous last meal together and descended from the upper city to the pool of Siloam and then through the gate, and down into the Kidron valley. It was a sombre procession, each of us lost in our own thoughts. Jesus was silent. As we threaded our way up the valley, the Temple Mount towering over us on our left, we passed a number of rough tombs carved out of the rock face, bathed in an eerie light. They weren't a happy addition to our walk.

We reached the garden where Jesus said he wanted to pray. It was called Gethsemane, and we had often used it as a place of rest and peace away from the noisy chaos of the city. How we needed that rest and peace now! We went in and flopped on the ground, tired well beyond the exertion of the walk. Still no-one spoke. Then Jesus said quietly that he wanted to go off by himself to pray. And he added, 'Pray that you won't come to the time of trial.' It was an odd phrase, and I wasn't entirely sure what he meant. Did he mean the immediate test we might face, perhaps tonight, with evil on the prowl? Or did he mean some bigger trial that Jerusalem and the Temple would face, as he'd said in the Temple the other day when it had sounded so strange, surrounded by all the massive stones and the security of the centuries? Or did he even mean the trial as something cosmic, with the end of everything and the return of the Son of Man—all of which had scared us enough then, let alone now?

He walked off slowly, picking his way round the sturdy olive trees and coming to a point where a great rock seemed to offer a natural place to kneel. I hope I didn't do wrong, but I felt compelled to follow quietly and—I don't know—*guard* him, or something. I couldn't let him go into this darkness alone. I sat down some yards away, but I caught the tenor of Jesus' prayer. He was deep in communion with his Abba, his Father, and praying that if there was another way, if he could be relieved of the awful prospect he saw ahead, please let it happen, let the bitter cup be taken away. (I suppose he was thinking of Abraham taking Isaac to be sacrificed on the mountain and being stopped at the last moment. Could there be a 'last moment' like that for Jesus?) And yet, if not, let it be. And I could see the sweat glistening on Jesus' neck and plastering his hair. When he moved his head to the side it looked as if the sweat was drops of blood.

It was too much. I realized I shouldn't be there; it was like listening in to the most intimate conversation between lovers. I crept away and sank to the ground next to the others, suddenly realizing they were asleep. It didn't take me long to join them. I suppose it was a combination of night-time, wine, and heavy emotion; we were gone . . .

. . . until suddenly Jesus was with us and our scrambled brains hurried to reorganize themselves. It was still dark; no dawn light to banish the nightmare of last night. It was still as before, all of it still true. Jesus spoke in hushed tones, without blame, but he asked why we were sleeping. 'Keep praying,' he said. 'Pray that you won't come to the time of trial.' Oh yes, that too was real.

Then we heard the sound of movement coming through the valley—the jangling of steel, the swish of legs through long grass, an occasional cough—and before we knew it, a band of sullen, determined-looking men were right in front of us. We struggled to our feet, still half in thrall to sleep. Then my blood went cold. In the middle of this unpleasant group of men was our friend Judas, and he was about to step forward, looking as if he was going to identify Jesus in the dark.

Jesus was strangely calm. He looked at Judas with a steady gaze. 'Are you going to betray me with a kiss, Judas?' he asked, wanting him to know what he was doing. If I had been Judas, all my life would have passed before me, all my commitment to the cause, my zeal for the kingdom, the vision we'd shared, the trust Jesus had put in me. Judas swayed, bewildered. But all of a sudden, violence broke out. Someone in our group had swiped a person in the crowd with one of the swords we had (it turned out to be one of the high priest's slaves, who lost his ear). But Jesus quickly stepped in. 'No more of this!' he said, and then, amazingly, he touched the man's ear and healed him. Who else but Jesus would have done that? True to the end.

The end? That's what it began to feel like. Jesus still wanted his accusers to take responsibility for their actions. He reminded them that they could have come and arrested him all week when he'd been teaching in the Temple. Why hadn't they? They couldn't admit it was because he was so popular with the people, but that was the truth. Equally true was what Jesus said next as the rope was pulled tight around his hands.

'But this is your hour, and the power of darkness.'

> *I wonder whether the disciples prayed during this evening, as well as Jesus?*
>
> *I wonder if there was ever a possibility that Jesus might have cut and run?*
>
> *I wonder what would have been the best and the worst thing you might have done in all this had you been a disciple?*
>
> *I wonder if you've ever been powerless in the hands of other people?*

Wednesday

Denial: Luke 22.54–62

It was a still, velvet night as the ragged group of priests, Temple police, and religious elders started back down into the Kidron valley. The sound of them receded into the distance, and suddenly I found I was alone. Where had all my friends gone? I could see Peter, bless him, following the crowd, unable to leave his best friend. But I was still standing in the garden, stunned. A moment ago I had witnessed the arrest of the man in whom I had placed all my hopes for three wonderful, upside-down years. I had come to see so many things the other way round— who was rich and who was poor, who was last and who was first, how to love my enemies and make them my friends, how to enjoy God rather than to fear him. My life had been transformed. I didn't know what I'd be doing in ten years' time, but I'd assumed it would be with Jesus.

But now? I was alone in a garden with a memory, and the reality that shaped my life had been dragged off to goodness knows what fate. I had to follow. Peter was already on the way, but I needed to keep separate from him; we had to keep in the background and not be noticed. I racked my sluggish brain to think where they might take Jesus in the middle of the night. They couldn't take him to the council at this hour; that would have to wait until morning. Perhaps, then, they would take him to Caiaphas's house? Yes, most likely. They'd keep him there and then bring him to the whole council the next day.

I suppose I should admit it now. I knew the high priest slightly—it's a long story. But I knew that should enable me to get into Caiaphas's courtyard and see what was happening. I set off, taking a different route from the crowd—I didn't want to be suspected of being a follower. (Why not? Was I ashamed of him? Scared? Or could I just not work it all out right now?) I arrived at the closed gate of the house quite a while after they must have gotten there and found a familiar shape waiting in the shadows. It was Peter. I whispered that I'd get him in, but we shouldn't show we knew each other.

So that's what we did. Inside, a warm fire was crackling away as servants wound their way through the crowd of priests, scribes, Temple police, and hangers-on, delivering drinks and small plates of egg, cheese, and olives. I stood back, leaning against a wall, slowly eating one of the snacks because I couldn't think what else to do. But Peter went and sat right by the fire where the glow showed up his drawn features. After a while one of the servant girls looked closely at this morose figure by the fire and said loudly, 'You were with that man they've just arrested. You're one of them!' Peter looked up angrily. 'I've never met him,' he snapped. I watched, aghast. Peter seemed to shrink into himself. A few minutes later another person who'd been looking at Peter fixedly declared, 'You really are one of them; you must be.' Peter looked alarmed. 'I told you, I'm nothing to do with him,' he half shouted, but he sounded too defensive to be telling the truth.

I willed Peter to back off and move away, but he was stubborn, or maybe just exhausted. His loyalty had brought him right into enemy territory, but as the night wore on shock and tiredness were causing his resolve to wane. It must have been an hour later when yet another person took a long look at Peter and declared, 'You were with him; you're a Galilean like him. I'd recognize that accent anywhere.' Peter stood up, knocking his stool over, and shouted furiously at the man, 'I don't know what the hell you're talking about!' And a cock crowed. In my memory everything froze for a few seconds. My befuddled brain refused to work.

But at that moment (I can hardly bear to remember it), they brought Jesus through the courtyard, presumably from an interrogation room to an overnight cell, and Jesus heard Peter's desperate denial. He must have heard it. And he turned and looked at Peter. But he looked with sorrow, not with blame. He knew what Peter was made of—rock—but rock can shatter too. Peter pushed his way out of the courtyard. He came close to where I was standing, and I could see the tears pouring down his face. It was tragic. Peter, our rock-man, reduced to a pile of rubble.

I didn't follow. Self-protection too, I guess. But I wanted to stay close to Jesus, even if I too had slunk into the shadows. And I felt terrible for him. He'd been betrayed by a close friend, denied by his most loyal follower, abandoned by his team of disciples, and now he was facing the full might of the religious authorities and probably the political authorities too. Tomorrow was a day full of threat. The possibilities were too dreadful to contemplate.

And he was alone, absolutely alone.

> *I wonder where the other disciples went and what they thought they should do next?*
> *I wonder if there might have been any danger that Peter would do what Judas did and kill himself after denying Jesus?*
> *I wonder where in Jerusalem you would be at this point in the story if you were one of the disciples?*
> *I wonder if you've had an experience of being disowned or of disowning someone else?*

Maundy Thursday

————•◦•————

Judgment: Luke 22.63—23.25

I went through the next few hours in a daze. For one thing I, was by myself for the first time for some years. We'd always been together, James and I, since birth, but Peter, Andrew, Thomas, and the rest of the lads as well, we were always a team, supporting Jesus. And now I was alone, trying to follow what was happening to the man I'd built my life around. But mainly I was in a daze because I couldn't believe what was happening. I hung around Caiaphas's courtyard long enough to hear unpleasant sounds coming from the cell where they'd taken Jesus. They must have blindfolded him because I heard them saying, 'Come on, big guy. You're a prophet—who hit you?' It was disgusting, and eventually I couldn't stand it anymore and wandered out into the dark streets.

I don't know where I went that night. I must have slept somewhere, probably under some tree or other, completely exhausted and wrung out. But the next thing I remember is being back at Caiaphas's house as the council gathered in the large open courtyard. It was what they called the Sanhedrin, with representatives of all the different religious authorities. Of course I couldn't get in to this bit, but I learned later what happened from one of the friendly Pharisees who knew that what was going on was wrong. And he said it was the chief priests, the scribes, and the elders who made most of the running, not really the Pharisees and Sadducees. But those chief priests really went for Jesus. Basically they wanted to get him to claim to be the Messiah so that they could go to Pilate and say he was a danger to Rome and had to be eliminated.

But it wasn't even a trial. There were no witnesses, no formal charges, no real condemnation, just mob rule disguised as legitimate inquiry. My contact said they asked him if he was the Messiah, and he turned it back on them and said, 'You say I am.' I could just imagine him doing that. He wanted them to take responsibility for their own interpretation of who he was, but he did make it easier for them by saying that the Son of Man (that strange figure again) would from now on be seated at the right hand of God. Anyway, they reckoned they had enough material to get him condemned, so they dragged Jesus off to Pilate, the only one who could give him a death sentence.

It was quite a walk to get to the Antonia Fortress, right across the city. This was where Pilate often stayed when he came up to Jerusalem from his house at Caesarea on the coast. He was out of his depth in all the intense religious politics of Jerusalem, so he hid himself away in his secure Roman world. I paced up and down outside, but my friendly Pharisee was there for it all. He said it was a fascinating and tragic event. Pilate was flustered, so he went in with a single blunt question which showed the heart of his own concerns. 'So are you the king of the Jews? Because if you are, you're a danger to Rome.' Jesus said again what he'd said to the council, 'You say so. What do you think?' This baffled Pilate. He wasn't unintelligent, but he was basically a Roman soldier used to fighting enemies, so he wanted black-and-white answers. 'I can't see the problem,' he said, but Jesus' accusers blustered even more about him stirring people up all over the place. Even Pilate knew that wasn't true. Jesus had never talked about driving the Romans into the sea. His followers hadn't risen in the streets when he was arrested; they'd vanished. And they had only two swords between them.

So Pilate said, 'I'll tell you what. You say he's a Galilean. It so happens that Herod Antipas, who looks after Galilee for us, is in town. I'll send this so-called revolutionary to Herod to see what he makes of him.' Now this was a truly sad encounter. It was between a man of real stature and a pathetic little bully. Herod was a joke to most of us, but a dangerous one. Apparently he'd been wanting to meet Jesus for some time to see who this charismatic young preacher was and to get him to perform some tricks, like walking across his swimming pool. Jesus simply wouldn't respond to such nonsense, and eventually Herod got so frustrated he tried to humiliate him, dressing him up as a royal figure and sending him back to Pilate in disgust. One interesting sidelight to all this was that apparently Pilate and Herod became fast friends after that, having been quite the opposite before. It was ironic; reconciliation couldn't help breaking out when Jesus was around.

When Jesus returned to Pilate I was able to get in to the fortress courtyard because the governor invited not only the chief priests and other religious leaders but also the ordinary people, so that this awkward little episode could be settled publicly. Pilate again tried to dismiss the case, saying that neither he nor Herod could see the problem and all it needed was for Jesus to be thoroughly flogged and then we could all get on with life.

But the crowd had been worked up by the religious leaders while Jesus was with Herod and they were incensed at this suggestion. They wanted Barabbas released, not Jesus. Now Barabbas was a nasty piece of work, a revolutionary who wanted to create mayhem and wasn't afraid of murdering people. And here was Jesus, a genuine revolutionary who wanted to bring peace, compassion, and justice and wasn't afraid of healing people and telling them they were of infinite value. What a choice! But they wanted Barabbas.

Pilate finally broke. He was a weak man, and he just wanted to get through his time as governor and get out of Palestine with all its ridiculous religious problems. The last thing he needed was word to get back to Rome that he'd allowed a silly dispute to become a full-scale storm. 'Have it your way,' he said. 'Crucify him.'

It was like a hammer blow. I collapsed onto a nearby step. How could it have come to this? In some absurd way I wanted us all to start again, to go back to the warm shores and gentle hills of Galilee, to feel the freedom as we walked those sunlit roads and shared the delight of the people as they listened to Jesus and were healed of so much illness. I wanted the camaraderie, the serious discussion, the practical jokes, the vision of a new nation, a new world.

But that dream had crumbled to dust. What lay ahead was a nightmare.

I wonder why Pilate was so weak?

I wonder if this crowd calling for Jesus to be crucified had any overlap with the crowd that had welcomed him on Palm Sunday or listened to him in the Temple?

I wonder why Jesus was so quiet?

I wonder if religious and political authorities are always inclined to get rid of awkward prophets?

Good Friday

Death: Luke 23.26–49

I don't know if I can manage the next part of the story. It's carved on my mind with a jagged knife. It hurts every time I go near it. But, as I now see, it's the very heart of everything—why Jesus came, what he had to do, what opened the door and let in all the light. But at the time there was no light at all for either me or the friends and family of Jesus who gathered quietly at the cross when we knew we had to be there.

They turfed Jesus out onto the narrow street, thronged with pilgrims for the festival. I stumbled out too, wanting somehow by my presence to take some of the weight of the cross from him. (What kind of foolishness was that?) But someone did in fact do just that. The crossbeam that Jesus had to carry was a foul, dark beast of a thing, far too heavy for a victim to support, already weak and scared as any victim would be. It landed on Jesus' shoulder with an agonizing crunch. He staggered, regained his balance, and then set off unsteadily. He clearly wasn't going to make it, and when the crossbeam crashed to the ground again, taking Jesus with it, the sweaty, overweight centurion pulled Simon from Cyrene out of the crowd. Simon was just in from the fields, making his way home, but his strong physique and dark skin marked him out, and he suddenly found he was at the center of the action. It's wonderful to hear his sons, Alexander and Rufus, talking about the change in their father's life brought about by those next few minutes—there's a whole story there that needs telling.

Jesus staggered on, with Simon taking as much weight as he could. I willed them on as I pushed my way through the uncaring crowd. Jesus managed a few words with a group of women crying their laments, but it was touch-and-go whether he would make it to the pitiful hill just outside the city gate where criminals were subjected to the worst death the Romans could devise. That death was slow and excruciatingly painful, sometimes going on for days as the victim gradually lost the struggle to push and pull himself up on the nails in order to breathe. He died of asphyxiation; and in humiliation, naked, cursed, and alone. The fear of those going to the cross can't begin to be imagined.

What was going through the mind of Jesus when the nails were being hammered through his wrists and feet as he was laid out on the unforgiving wood? I've no idea. But I guess there was a clue when he suddenly spoke his first words for a long time, whispering a prayer that his Father would forgive these people because they didn't know what they were doing. It was astonishing that he should pray for his torturers like that. I was only a few yards away at the time, so I can vouch for it. And it inspired other friends of ours in the difficult days to come—Stephen, for example, was martyred with similar words on his lips.

I couldn't keep away, but every moment was agony—though the merest outer edge of what it was like for him. That demonic cross was first raised and then dropped with a practised thud into its familiar hole, jolting Jesus' whole body agonizingly. You could see the mist of pain dull his eyes. Then he rallied a bit and tried to focus and see who was there for him. I looked around too and saw Mary, broken beyond belief, and a few of the others creeping back silently to witness the death of their dreams.

What hurt even more were the cruel taunts of the leaders who had done this, and the soldiers who offered him vinegar, and even one of the criminals alongside him. They all had this theme that if Jesus really was this 'Messiah', this 'King of the Jews' (it was what the inscription over him said), if he really could save others, why didn't he save himself? It was the same temptation he had faced in the wilderness a lifetime ago: 'If you are the Son of God . . .' Most of the time Jesus was far away in a world of his own, but when the other criminal being crucified remonstrated with his thoughtless partner-in-crime, Jesus roused himself and turned an exhausted smile on him and said he would be with Jesus in Paradise that very day. It was the promise of an angel. But there was much more to go through first.

It began to get dark. That was truly odd because it had been a fine day. It seemed to my fevered imagination that the powers of evil were wrapping themselves around us, or maybe that nature itself was participating in the drama on the hill. I was told later that the curtain in the Temple that divided the holy of holies from the holy place had been torn apart mysteriously at the same hour. These were strange times indeed.

But then the inevitable happened. Jesus' breathing got more labored and desperate. Each breath was torn out of him as he struggled for survival. We heard one last message come from his dying lips, words that were somehow full and reassuring in the midst of my emotional chaos: 'Here is my spirit, Father. You take care of it now.' And his head fell onto his chest. There was no more movement, no more sound. Life had gone out of him.

There was silence.

Then a single bird started singing its heart out. I was trans-fixed. The centurion, the same one who had dragged Simon out of the crowd a few hours ago, was also spellbound. He was looking at the bloody, peaceful body of Jesus, and he dared to say with absolute conviction, to no one in particular: 'This man was undoubtedly innocent.' And he filled the word 'innocent' with far more meaning than it usually contained. Meanwhile those of us from Galilee who had feasted on life in the company of Jesus and tasted the sweet wine of the kingdom at his hand, looked on, unable to think, unable to move, unable to weep.

He'd gone.

> *I wonder what it was that Simon of Cyrene experienced that day that made such a difference to him?*
>
> *I wonder why Jesus died so much faster than was usually the case?*
>
> *I wonder what the friends and family of Jesus did to regroup after this disaster?*
>
> *I wonder how you are left feeling after you've stood and gazed at the cross for a while?*

Holy Saturday poem

'A song for the tomb' by Teresa Morgan

Ages before Jerusalem was founded
I was formed for this day.
God said, shall these sea-bones live?
I will sculpt me a tomb: a lime-white chamber
fit for a king.

I was ready when they brought him in:
bloody and broken, like a king from his last
battle. Dusk was falling. They hurried, careful.
So careful. They were brittle with pain.
They straightened him (legs, arms, head) in the niche;
stopped my mouth with a rock, and crept away.

We were quiet together.
He slept inside me. I cradled him,
like a child unborn. Outside,
Earth shuddered; the sun failed; stars shot like bolts
Through warring heavens.
I kept him safe

til he began to stir
like the child whose time has come.
The deep places of creation whispered,
Let there be light!
A mighty spasm shook the stone. I gaped.
He rose. For a moment
he stood facing the dawn, then he was gone.

Later
there would be angels, blazing-eyed
and docile, folding linen bandages.
There would be men and women, storms of grieving
suddenly stilled.
But first, as the sun rose,
there was just light and silence. A cave empty
and a world full of promises fulfilled.

> *I wonder how you responded to this unusual perspective on
> the resurrection?*
> *I wonder which phrases caught your attention?*
> *I wonder which words and phrases that aren't in the poem
> you associate with the resurrection?*
> *I wonder what difference the resurrection makes to your
> faith day by day?*

After Easter

Another journey: Luke 24.13–35

This was the story we heard from our friends Cleopas and Mary. I'll tell it as faithfully as I can.

It was late afternoon, and they were trudging out to Emmaus. They were physically exhausted and emotionally in pieces. They didn't say much to each other. They knew what was in each other's heart, the dull ache, the disillusion, the memories of the dreams now strewn along the road behind them. Seven miles wasn't a long journey, but it was as if each step was on sharp stones.

It was over. The great romance, the Galilean dream, the high tide of hope through the last week; it was all over. How could it have fallen apart so quickly? Only a week ago they had been pouring down the Mount of Olives and up into the city, carried on a wave of goodwill, ready to take on the world. And now the world, the real world, had trapped them, chewed them up, and spit them out.

The conversation was desultory. They rehearsed the events in broken pieces. They hadn't been part of the Twelve, but they'd been caught up in the momentum of this exciting teacher/prophet. They'd been entranced by Jesus: they'd hung on his words; they'd loved his teaching—and been convicted by it too. If he brought this teaching to Jerusalem, there was no limit to what might happen. Surely his exciting vision of the kingdom of God would capture every heart.

How could they have been so naive?

They needed to get out, to get some space. They didn't say this to each other, but they feared for their own safety too. What if a roundup was going on even now? The other friends and followers of Jesus had gone to ground. Only some of the women were brave enough to have prepared spices to preserve the body this morning. Jerusalem wasn't safe.

It was then that they realized someone had quietly caught up with them and fallen in step beside them. The sun was low and cast its golden glow over the long road; it was hard to make out his features, but he seemed friendly enough. He asked what they had been talking about. And that finally brought them to a halt. The strength suddenly emptied out of them, and they gave up the pretence of being all right, of being two ordinary travelers going home after a day or two in the city.

When Cleopas found his words, they were more sarcastic than he had meant, but he had no defenses against his grief. 'Are you the only person in the whole of Jerusalem who doesn't know what's gone on this weekend?' 'Tell me,' said the other.

So they did. It helped to tell the whole story again. To remind themselves of the chronology, the people, the places. But when it came to Jesus being dragged off and hammered onto a bloody cross, there to die by inches, Cleopas stumbled to a halt. 'And we had thought he was the one who was going to redeem Israel,' he muttered, confused, hurt, and embarrassed all at the same time.

Summoning up a few shreds of memory, he ventured a little more. Rumors had started to circulate that the women who had taken the spices that morning had found the tomb empty and they'd seen a vision of angels or something and said that Jesus was alive. But of course the women in the group were understandably very emotional at the moment, and you couldn't trust any of these wild stories. Anyway, the women didn't see Jesus themselves.

'So here we are. Going home. It's over,' said Cleopas. He and Mary, his wife, stood together in the evening light, heads down, as forlorn on the outside as they were dejected within.

It was a bit of a surprise, then, when after a few moments of silence the stranger said quietly, 'You fools!' They looked at him. Fortunately he was smiling. 'You've been a bit slow, haven't you? Slow to see that the Messiah really did have to suffer like that?'

And as they started walking again, slowly but purposefully toward Emmaus, this enigmatic stranger began to unfold the Scriptures in a way that was simply electrifying. It was as if he was cleaning away a layer of dark paint and revealing the original picture underneath, glowing in its original colors. The clues were all there, from the Passover to the prophets. People thought God would redeem Israel *from* suffering, whereas actually God would redeem Israel *through* suffering. The Messiah would have to take Israel's suffering onto himself. It was an amazing experience to see the whole story of God's love re-imagined and to hear it restated so clearly. As Cleopas said to Mary later, 'Didn't our hearts burn within us as he explained the Scriptures?'

The sun was very low when they reached Emmaus, the shadows reaching far back toward Jerusalem. They stopped outside Cleopas and Mary's house, and the stranger was saying his good-byes, when Cleopas knew instinctively that it was wrong. He must ask the stranger to stay and have a meal with them. He was deeply moved by what they had just heard. In any case, simple hospitality demanded a more generous response.

It started as a normal meal—fairly frugal, given the circumstances, but there was bread and cheese and wine and fruit. They carried on talking about the events of the last few days and the fresh meaning that was beginning to emerge. Cleopas was obviously the host, but toward the end of the meal an odd shift began to take place, and it seemed as if the stranger was becoming the host. He took bread from the dish, held it up in thanksgiving, broke it, and gave it to the others.

And for Cleopas and Mary, everything started to spin, reality lurched sideways, and the world shifted on its axis.

When they had gathered their scattered wits from the four corners, the stranger was no longer there. They looked at each other, mouths open. Was it ... could it ... did it just ...? Yes, yes, yes! They shot out of the house, tired limbs made new, and raced back along the road on which they had so recently ploughed their sad path. But now all was lightness and amazement and joy, and the desperate need to tell the others. Who cared what the dangers were? There was a new story to tell and a new fire burning within them.

After they got back to Jerusalem, they talked about it with the others far into the night. There was an air of unreality, certainly, but also a feeling of limitless possibility. Friends and followers of Jesus kept appearing, having heard the rumors, and each time Cleopas and Mary, and Peter and the women had to tell their stories again. The room became increasingly crowded and alight with feverish excitement. They had no idea what to do next, but that wasn't the point. They already had more than enough to cope with.

As they talked on in subsequent days and weeks, they began to see so many things falling into place. The meal Cleopas and Mary had shared felt somehow like the first meal of a new creation, echoing the first meal of the old Creation that had gone wrong when the woman gave the fruit to her husband in the Garden of Eden. The new meal and the way Jesus did it seemed set to be a key event for them all to continue in the future—a common celebration, a communion. And Mary had a remarkable thought too. She remembered Jesus' parents and their three days desperately searching for him, years before, when he'd stayed behind talking to teachers in the Temple. Now she and Cleopas had been repeating that event, another couple desperately searching for Jesus, mentally and spiritually, for another three days. And in both cases he would have said he had been 'doing my Father's work'. So there was the same pattern at the beginning and the end of Jesus' life.

That was getting a bit fanciful perhaps, but what they truly knew was that they were on the brink of a new world, a new life. The deep engines of Creation had been thrown into reverse. Death had been delivered a fatal blow. There was everything to play for.

But as John said, 'What on earth happens now?'

> *I wonder if we think of Cleopas and Mary (a presumption based on John 19.25) as being part of the much larger group surrounding Jesus (Acts 1.15), and if so, I wonder how these people related to the disciples?*
>
> *I wonder if you've ever felt similarly downhearted about your faith? And what happened then?*
>
> *I wonder if Christ is 'made known to [us] in the breaking of the bread'?*
>
> *I wonder what impact the resurrection has on our lives now?*

Using The Journey to Jerusalem *in a group*

Here's a straightforward way to use the sections of this book during Lent, or at any other time.

1 Select the passage or passages for reflection. If the group is meeting once a week in Lent, you might choose one or two from the previous week (if possible, give the group members advance warning the week before).

2 Read aloud the passage from Luke and allow at least three minutes of silence for group members to reflect quietly on it.

3 Read aloud the section from *The Journey to Jerusalem* and allow at least five minutes for members to start pondering the 'I wonder' questions. These periods of time always seem longer than they are—don't hurry them and the group will quickly get used to them and value them.

4 Then go through the 'I wonder' questions either as a full group or, if the numbers suggest, in pairs first, before doing so in the full group.

5 If two passages have been selected, repeat the process.

6 Ask if there are any other 'wonderings' that emerged in members' minds that haven't been covered in the discussion.

7 Take the wonderings into prayer, which could be: (a) open prayer; (b) prayer prepared by the leader; (c) Compline/Night Prayer; (d) silence. Music is often a rich addition to a time of reflection.